William Cosmo Monkhouse

The Studies of Sir Edwin Landseer, R.A.

William Cosmo Monkhouse

The Studies of Sir Edwin Landseer, R.A.

ISBN/EAN: 9783742834133

Manufactured in Europe, USA, Canada, Australia, Japa

Cover: Foto ©Thomas Meinert / pixelio.de

Manufactured and distributed by brebook publishing software
(www.brebook.com)

William Cosmo Monkhouse

The Studies of Sir Edwin Landseer, R.A.

THE STUDIES

OF

SIR EDWIN LANDSEER, R.A.

ILLUSTRATED BY SKETCHES

FROM THE

COLLECTION OF HER MAJESTY THE QUEEN

AND OTHER SOURCES

WITH A HISTORY OF HIS ART-LIFE

BY

W. COSMO MONKHOUSE

LONDON

VIRTUE AND COMPANY, Limited, 26, IVY LANE

PATERNOSTER ROW

THE Publishers of "Landseer's Studies" embrace this opportunity to return their respectful thanks to HER MOST GRACIOUS MAJESTY THE QUEEN; HIS GRACE THE DUKE OF WESTMINSTER; Messrs. THOMAS AGNEW & SONS; F. A. MILBANK, Esq., M.P.; J. FOWLER, Esq.; H. W. F. BOLCKOW, Esq., M.P.; Messrs. GRAVES; C. W. MANSEL LEWIS, Esq.; GEO. GURNEY, Esq.; J. CLARK, Esq.; C. WILSON, Esq.; H. KETTEL, Esq.; J. KNIGHT, Esq.; J. WEDDERBURN, Esq.; A. HARRIS, Esq.; Messrs. HAY & SON; F. PIERCY, Esq.; Mrs. ARTHUR LEWIS; W. WALKER, Esq.; DR. PICK; H. VAUGHAN, Esq.; the DIRECTORS OF THE SOUTH KENSINGTON MUSEUM; P. FLETCHER WATSON, Esq.; RAFFAELLE C. ISAAC, Esq.; JAS. DAFFORNE, Esq.; Rev. C. M. E. COLLINS; Messrs. NICHOLLS; C. G. LEWIS, Esq.; H. G. REID, Esq.; W. J. ALLEN, Esq.; H. CROXFORD, Esq.; J. PAGE, Esq.; the EXECUTORS OF CAPTAIN PALMER; FULLER MAITLAND, Esq.; A. MYERS, Esq.; H. KING SPARK, Esq.; W. LETHBRIDGE, Esq.; Mrs. NOSEDA; DR. BOYD; W. P. BODKIN, Esq.; R. RAWLINSON, Esq., C.B.; R. NAPIER, Esq.; H. A. SPARKE, Esq.; and Messrs. MAWSON, SWAN AND MARSTON, for their great courtesy in contributing to this interesting Volume, by the loan of the Illustrations by which alone its production has been rendered possible.

CONTENTS.

LIST OF ILLUSTRATIONS.

PLATES.

c

FIG. 1.—IN THE PASTURE (1810).

LANDSEER'S STUDIES.

CHAPTER I.

1808—16.

FOR the boy who, at the age of eight, could sketch from nature the little group of sheep with which this chapter is headed a career had evidently been marked out by Nature, if he chose to follow her guidance. There are observable in it not only a careful imitation of the animals, but considerable skill in drawing, observation of character and habit, a certain instinct of composition, and management of light and shade, and many other qualities which are never seen in the work of a boy, unless that boy be like Landseer was—an artist born. But, as will be seen by a comparison of the date placed under the cut on the next page, he had attained some mastery with the pencil at least a year before he drew these sheep. It was when six or seven years old, *i.e.* in 1808 or 1809, according to a memorandum by Miss Eliza Meteyard, published in Mr. Stephens's interesting memoirs of the artist, that his father, John Landseer, who was not only a good engraver, but a writer and lecturer upon Art and archæology, made him sketch a cow from nature in a field on the Finchley Road.* It was probably not far from this field that the sheep were drawn, as this became for some years afterwards his favourite sketching ground. Between his home in Foley Street and Hampstead, then open fields for the most part, the boy used to sketch till he was fetched by his father in the evening, who would criticize his work, and often make him correct it on the spot. He was therefore not only provided with natural talent, but with a natural studio and a

---

* He drew, however, and, according to Mr. Stephens, "drew well and studied animal character and humour thoroughly at the age of five."—Vide "Memoirs of Sir E. Landseer," by F. G. Stephens, p. 15. George Bell & Sons, 1874.

B

natural master, and he could scarcely have produced such good early work except with the joint assistance of the three.

But Landseer had an indoor as well as an outdoor studio, and this was Exeter Change. Here he used to go and sketch from the wild beasts which were then shown there. His earliest etching was made from a sketch by himself of a lion's head in profile, and on the same plate his brother Thomas, his elder by seven years, etched a head of a tiger drawn by Edwin, also in profile. Nature thus provided him, from his earliest years, with an engraver, and one who was peculiarly fitted to interpret his work.

FIG. 2.—LIONESS AND CUBS (1809).

Among all his many engravers there is none who has engraved so many of his works as his brother Thomas, and none who has shown such sympathy with his style and touch and feeling. Far more extraordinary as a design, though not as a piece of manipulative skill, is the drawing of a "Lioness and Cubs" (Fig. 2), of which we give a woodcut. Though very defective in drawing, there is great vigour in the attitude of the lioness, and a true sense of the cubby spirit in her offspring, especially in the cub which is trying to get on its mother's back. Whether this was entirely a study from the life is doubtful. The composition, notwithstanding the proof we have of Landseer's

Senegal Lion from Exeter Change in 1811 drawn by Edwin Landseer aged nine years

SENEGAL LION (1811).

IN THE JUNGLE (1811).

PLATE I.

precocity, seems impossible for a child of seven, and there is much similarity between the head of this lioness and that of a lioness in a picture by Stubbs, now in the Museum at South Kensington. There is, however, no reason for thinking that it was copied, any more than the vigorous, but also badly drawn, design of " In the Jungle," the lower illustration in PLATE I. It seems certain that his imagination, especially in connection with wild beasts, was exercised early, or he could not have produced his pictures of " A Lion enjoying his Repast " and " A Lion disturbed at his Repast," which were exhibited at the Royal Academy in 1820, or the undoubtedly original and masterly composition of the " Contending Group of Leopard, Tiger, and Lion," which was engraved by his brother Thomas, and published in 1823 in a volume entitled

FIG. 3 —STUDY OF A LION (1812).

" Twenty-six Engravings of Lions, Tigers, Panthers, and Leopards, by Stubbs, Rembrandt, Spilsbury, Reydinger, and Edwin Landseer, with an Essay on the Carnivora, by J. Landseer."

The other drawings of lions which adorn this chapter, viz. " The Senegal Lion from Exeter Change," * at the top of PLATE I., and the " Study of a Lion " (Fig. 3), belonging to Mr. Dafforne, are also singularly remarkable, and for opposite reasons: the first from the evident faithfulness of the study, and from its likeness in attitude and statuesque calm to the last and greatest of his achievements in this direction—the

* This lion was possibly the same animal as that from which he made two drawings in 1814, one of which was engraved by his brother Thomas, and the other by his father, and the name of which was " Nero." It is certain at all events that " Nero " was a Senegal Lion, and was exhibited at Exeter Change.

lions in Trafalgar Square; the latter as the first indication given, as far as we know, of the talent so often thereafter to be happily exercised of imbuing animals with a semi-human expression.   It appears here in its very earliest phase, probably born of the pleasure which we must all of us have felt in tracing a human likeness in other things, whether a cloud, a fire, or an animal.   Landseer cultivated it till he made it a specialty of his art, the source of many a quaint and humorous fancy, the barb of much good-natured satire, with the result of giving harmless pleasure to thousands who could not rise to the level of the pure poetry of his noblest work.

The sight of lions and tigers is only an incident in our lives, and the painting of

FIG. 4.—STUDIES IN A FARMYARD (1810).

them only an incident in Landseer's art, which was mainly devoted to the study of the form and character of the animals of his own country, especially those most closely connected with human life.   But it was far from an unimportant incident, as his early studies of wild beasts show, more distinctly perhaps than any other of his studies of wild life, that his imagination could be vigorously employed in realising what life is to animals, rather than what their life seems to us, and because they show an enthusiasm and a resolute struggle with difficulties, both of thought and execution, which contrast with the easy masterliness of most of his other work.   Of all wild beasts the lion laid the strongest hold upon his mind, and of all its qualities, real or ascribed, its power and its dignity. Whatever discoveries naturalists and travellers may make derogatory to the time-honoured character of the royal beast, his appearance, at least for the artist, and especially the British artist, will be a sufficient title to preserve his regard for ever as the type of natural nobility. Nor do we think it a transcendental notion that Landseer's early sympathy with and studies from the kingliest of animals

E. Landseer

FIG. 5.—STUDIES IN A FARMYARD (1810).

had much influence in forming the style of his art, of which breadth and simplicity, calmness and strength, courage and sincerity, are qualities which are never absent.

But we must now come back for a while to the little boy Edwin sketching in the fields near Hampstead, and returning home with his father to make his first essays in etching. We have mentioned his first etching, which was of a head of a lion; what was possibly his second, executed at the age of eight, was made from his own drawing

c

of heads of a donkey, sheep, and boar, in the possession of Mr. George Gurney. The woodcut which we give of this drawing, "Studies in a Farmyard," 1810 (Fig. 4), makes unnecessary any comments on the wonderful skill of the boy both in drawing and etching; but it may be observed with what truth the different characters of the animals are seized, especially the mixture of patience and anxiety in the profile of the sheep, and the sleepy sensuality of the boar. The other heads are studies of the manner in which the different animals approach their food with their lips. On page 5 will be

FIG. 6.—BAITING THE BULL (1810).

found another study of the art of eating, this time the animal is a cow; and another of a pig (Fig. 5), this time a female, sleeping. This and the following cut of "Baiting the Bull" (Fig. 6) belong to the same year (1810), together with the study of sheep which heads this chapter, and the study of donkeys which concludes it. Altogether these make a very fair sample of a year's work by a boy of eight, and show that his labours were not only well sustained, but well guided, all being directed towards one object, viz. the study of the life and character of animals.

It helped the boy to make sure and quick progress in his art that its object was always the same, without tentative efforts in other directions. Many artists, like the late John Philip, have to wait till middle age ere their special talent declares itself by meeting, by accident perhaps, with the class of subject in which alone they can achieve success. One man, after painting landscapes indifferently for years, will suddenly produce a portrait which will be as a beam of light to him, and show him his future path to fame; another, gifted with unusual power of pathos, will fruitlessly and with apparent perverseness waste the best part of his life in his desire to be a second Hogarth. Sometimes timidity, sometimes misdirected ambition, will make a man miss his proper path, but to most in early youth, before the mind is fully formed,

Fig. 7.—A Persian Cat (1810—11).

there is a period of hesitation, of comparative darkness, where the only thing certain is the presence of an artistic gift which impels its possessor to draw whatever presents itself to be drawn, without any marked preference for a special object. But with Landseer there was never any such indecision, no time wasted, no steps to be retraced, not even from imperfect guidance; his road was straight before him and not to be mistaken, and, as if to prevent any possibility of divergence, he had a father and a brother to guide him and to give him a helping hand.

The only thing wanting to point the foregoing observations is that his first study should have been a dog; and perhaps it was, but the dog in " Baiting the Bull," 1810 (Fig. 6), is his first drawing of that animal of which we have any note. This dog,

however, does not look like a first attempt, and though not so well drawn as the other
animals of the same year, shows more spirit than any. Its spirit is, we fear, more
certain than its breed, which is certainly not that of what we know as a thoroughbred
bulldog; perhaps when bulls were still baited the breed was different, or the dogs
actually used for baiting were not thoroughbred. If the head of the bovine animal
were not so unmistakably male, we should have been inclined to think the drawing
was meant to illustrate the house that Jack built, in which a dog whose breed is
unstated was tossed by a cow with a crumpled horn.

Dogs are restless animals, and unless asleep are not good sitters for portraits,
especially in the open air, where Landseer first studied. The lazy habits of sheep and
pigs and cattle in the fields, of cats indoors, and of wild beasts in cages, are sufficient

FIG. 8.—A RETRIEVER (1810—11).

reasons why these animals should form the subjects of Landseer's early studies, but
it is certain that if there had been at this time a dog in his home in Foley Street, he
would have drawn him as he did the cat. The cat was asleep, and was drawn by
him in 1809, and etched by Mr. Thomas Landseer in 1823.

We may, however, be mistaken in supposing that the cat of 1809 was a cat that
dwelt at Foley Street with himself and his family; it may have been a friend's cat, like
the one engraved from a drawing in the possession of the Rev. C. M. E. Collins,
which the artist has quaintly verified by the inscription, "Sketched at Maldon by the
little boy Edwin, when ten years old, now Sir E. Landseer, an old boy, 1866." This
sketch, "A Persian Cat" (Fig. 7), or rather drawing, for the attempt at finish is elaborate,
is, we think, more like a juvenile production than any of the earlier performances of
the artist of which we have given engravings. To say nothing of the very obvious

error in the drawing of the top of the stool on which pussy is sitting, there is a want
of life about it and a waste of work. It is more like a stuffed (and a badly stuffed)
animal than a live one, although the careful attempt to render the fur and to show
the formation of the body deserves praise. The same remarks will apply to the
drawing of "A Retriever" (Fig. 8), belonging to the same gentleman, where the same
ambition after finish observable in most young work ends in the same unfortunate result,
viz. a general flatness and lifelessness of effect. Here, however, the young artist
has been a little more successful, partly because his desire for definition is not so

FIG. 9.—STUDY OF GOATS (1811).

much balked by the fur, which, though longer than he knew quite well how to
manage, does not so completely disguise the anatomy of the animal.* As showing
the same difficulties, but partially conquered, our next illustration is interesting:
"Study of Goats," 1811 (Fig. 9), belonging to Mr. Gurney. In this, though the heads
and horns are well drawn, the bodies are shapeless and the legs stiff; defects due, we
think, in a great measure, to the long hair, which hides the framework and destroys

---

* These two drawings of the Persian Cat and Retriever were drawn at the house of Mr. W. W. Simpson,
of Maldon, where the young Edwin went for change of air. They were given by him to Lucy Potter, then in the
service of Mr. Simpson. See *Art Journal* for December, 1876.

outline. All these drawings show how impossible it is, even with the highest natural
gifts, to draw figures correctly without a knowledge of their anatomy, especially if, as
in the case of long-haired animals, nature has reduced the outward indications of her
design to the minimum. To take, for example, the earlier animals of Landseer which
illustrate this chapter; it will, we think, be found on comparison that their success is in
nearly inverse proportion to the length of their hair. All these considerations prove
to us that it was high time for the artist to begin to study anatomy, and that he
thought so too, and did it, is apparent from "An Anatomical Study," 1812 (Fig. 10),
belonging to Messrs. Graves, of the skull of a pointer, in the corner of which is

FIG. 10.—AN ANATOMICAL STUDY (1812).

probably the first well-drawn and well-modelled head of a dog which ever came from
his hand. The importance not only of anatomical drawing, but of dissection, was
enforced upon him the year after by the unfortunate Haydon.

Though Landseer seems to have drawn other animals before he attempted a dog,
and seems to have drawn them better at first, yet after he once began to draw dogs he
never rested till he had mastered them thoroughly, and they hereafter were to be his
favourite subjects throughout his life; but as we intend to devote a special chapter to
his treatment of these—the most human of animals, in spite of anatomy and Mr.
Darwin—we shall confine our remarks in this chapter to his progress in skill in drawing
them, and not further dwell upon his remarkable love for and sympathy with every

shade of the canine nature. That his study of anatomy was sincere and thorough is shown by the fact, recorded by Mr. Dafforne,* that "the margin of the paper on which the drawing ('An Anatomical Study') is made is covered with references to the different parts of the skull, and their proper anatomical names are given."

The dog in Fig. 11 ("Among the Turnips"), though in advance of the other dogs figured previously, is still very stiff and imperfect in drawing, and, though it bears the same date as the anatomical study, must surely have been drawn before it. The hand that had sketched the skull, and the life-like head above it, could never have been satisfied with this shapeless muzzle, unless indeed the subject were another *lusus naturæ* (see Fig. 12); and the disparity between the hind and fore quarters of the animal shows conclusively that his study of the anatomy of the animal had not

FIG. 11.—AMONG THE TURNIPS (1812).

extended with much result to the rest of the body. His growing interest in dogs is nevertheless shown by this painful effort to represent a setter in its characteristic attitude, and also by two other studies of the same year, entered in Mr. Graves's careful catalogue of Landseer's works: one of which is a portrait of "Racket," in the possession of Mr. Robert Rawlinson, C.B., which was exhibited in the collection of Landseer's works shown in 1874 at Burlington House; and the other a drawing of a "Brown Mastiff Sleeping," which was sold at Sir John Swinburne's sale in 1861 for seventy guineas.

Of his studies of cattle belonging (probably) to this early period none is more curious than that which is styled "A Lusus Naturæ" (Fig. 12), of which the original pencil sketch, like so many of those engraved in these pages, belongs to Mr. George

Gurney. Where did Landseer see this ? Was it tethered in a field near Hampstead,
or was it exhibited at a fair? We have ourselves seen an unfortunate beast of the
same kind with a similar excrescence, but there was no doubt in that case what the
excrescence was—viz. another and smaller pair of hind legs, with tail complete,
which depended in a ludicrous and pitiable manner from somewhere near the middle of
the unhappy creature's back. Mr. Dafforne* thinks that it must be "a cluster of
horns which nature, in one of her strangest freaks, has placed where they are." We,
however, remembering the monstrosity we have seen, are inclined to think that the

FIG. 12.—A LUSUS NATURÆ.

hideous outgrowth is in this case also superfluous hindquarters, the hoofs of which have
grown into the semblance of horns, and that its position is accounted for by stoppage
of its growth.

The next group that we give, though undoubtedly drawn from nature in England,
reminds us much more of the Dutch type of cattle, as drawn by Cuyp, than the animals
we are accustomed to see in our own fields. The drawing, "In the Meadow" (Fig. 13),
is remarkable for the pains taken to show the formations of the muscles, and the undu-
lations of the hides due to other causes. The characters of the beasts are also well

* *Art Journal*, January, 1876.

QUITE AT HOME (1813).

A SHORT-HORN BULL (1812).

PLATE II.

"differentiated"—the sturdy sullenness of the bull, and the bland passivity of his mate. Still finer is the "Short-horn Bull" (1812) at the bottom of PLATE II.—a brute of a higher order of intelligence, whom it would be dangerous to disturb from his selfish meditations. These two drawings were combined by Landseer (Edwin) in one etching, with fine effect, and nothing can illustrate better his natural skill in composition than these two drawings and the etching which combines them: it is difficult to say which

FIG. 13.—IN THE MEADOW.

of the three is the best balanced. On the same plate as this etching is another fine group of cattle.

We should, from our engraving, have been inclined to give even greater praise to the cat at the top of PLATE II., both from the great difficulty of drawing that animal and the apparently exquisite finish of its fur; but Mr. Dafforne informs us that it is taken from an oil-picture which has all the appearance of very juvenile handiwork; yet we are not sure that an oil-picture, capable of such a beautiful translation into black and white, is not a more wonderful achievement for a boy of eleven than his etchings of this period. The work shows at all events a great progress in two or three years since he

E

attempted to draw the " Persian Cat " (Fig. 7) at the house of his friend, Mr. W. W.
Simpson, at Maldon.   This animal is fully alive from the tip of its nose to the tip of
its tail, it is well put together, its attitude is easy and characteristic, its face intelligent,
and its form thoroughly understood.   Three years later (1816) he had mastered
even Persian cats, as is proved by the exquisite etchings by his brother Thomas of
" Head and Tail of a Persian Cat from Maldon " and " Persian Cats at a Window,"
of which we wish we were able to give impressions here.

In turning over these sketches, arranged as far as possible in chronological order,
it is curious to mark their inequality in execution : in one sketch he seems to have
arrived at mastery, in another he seems to have sunk back into pupilhood.   One thinks
at first that the sketches have been missorted, but on examination the dates affixed

FIG. 14 — A TOURNAMENT (1812).

are sufficient proof to the contrary, and reasons for the difference have to be sought
elsewhere.   They are generally discoverable either in the greater difficulty of the
subjects of the less successful attempts, as in the case of long-haired animals, upon
which we have already remarked, or in the fact that the subjects are new and have
been studied less.   It is not without pleasure that the conclusion is arrived at that the
boy, though unusually gifted, was a boy after all, and that the comparative value of his
work depended quite as much upon circumstances, and the comparative progress he
made quite as much upon application, as in the case of the dullest boys.   It is a very
refreshing discovery in connection with a young genius to find that his precocity is not .
abnormal, and that his development is natural and healthy.   Edwin Landseer, early as
his powers were cultivated, was no forced plant, no hothouse prodigy.   Though he could
soon produce work which had all the appearance of matured power, it was only within a

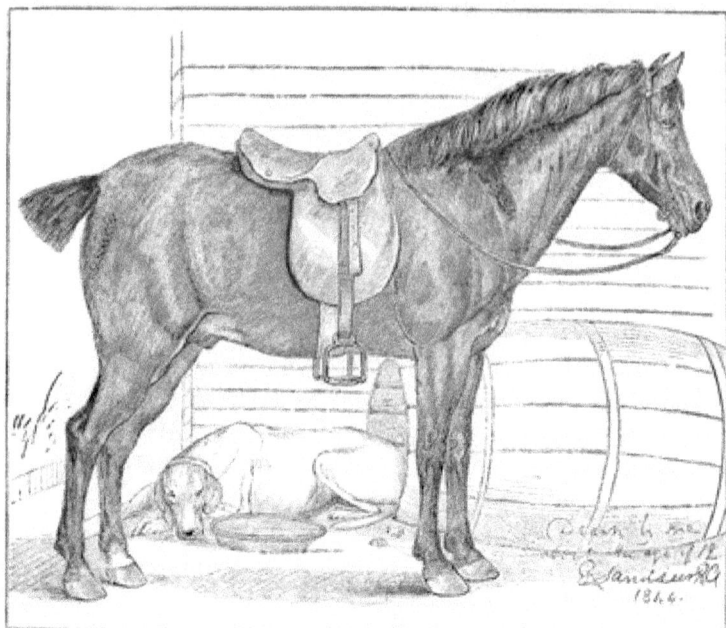

WAITING TO START (1814).

A FAVOURITE POINTER (1814).

PLATE III.

very limited range, and was simply the result of remarkable talent, combined with sound study, directed to the drawing of a few objects for which he had a natural predilection. He conquered his difficulties quicker than others, but they all had to be conquered. Details are wanting of his early life, but from what we do know, his work, if unusually steady for a boy of his age, was also performed under unusually healthy conditions. Instead of being cooped up in a room, his study was in the fields, and the subjects which he drew—the cows and the sheep, the donkeys and the dogs, even the lions and tigers—were such as are congenial and wholesome to the minds of all healthy boys, and were not likely to encourage the morbid activity of the intellect so often the fatal accompaniment of youthful prodigies.

That he retained all the love of fun, which such a curly-headed youngster as he

FIG. 15.—SHEEP-SHEARING (1813).

was should, is sufficiently plain from the sketch of " The Tournament " (Fig. 14), in which a hideous demon, in a military costume humorously unsuited to his wings and tail, is with a savage expression of delight pinning exactly through the middle of his breast-plate a being half-knight and half-fiend. What the meaning of this terrible encounter may be will probably never be known, but the drawing is remarkable for its spirit, especially the figure of the vanquished devil who is throwing up his arms and falling back. There is real power in the way his helpless agony is expressed by the curling of the talons of his feet : those of the left foot being curled downwards as if to grip the ground, those of the right curling upwards in sheer pain and despair. This was selected out of a number of juvenile sketches sold among the *débris* of the artist's studio after his death.* This is the first drawing of anything like a human form of which we have any note.

In the next year, 1813,† the drawing of " Sheep-shearing " (Fig. 15) gives visible proof that he had begun to add to his studies of farm life those of men. A very careful study is this of a man engaged in the delicate operation of shearing, but bearing evident traces of an early attempt, especially in the foreshortening of the right arm and the drawing of the hands and face. Contrasted with the few clever touches with which a terrier's head is sketched in the corner of the same figure, it shows at once how much more study he had given to animals than to men, and also, we think, how much more natural aptitude he had for catching expression in animals than in men. As in this, his first drawing of the human figure, so in all, with a few remarkable exceptions, half-a-dozen touches of an animal would convey more interest and be more

FIG. 16.—ASLEEP (1814).

full of artistic meaning than all the pains he could bestow upon a human subject; from which it must not be gathered that we wish to undervalue his power in representing human beings, which was considerable, if more limited.

Our next drawing, "Asleep" (Fig. 16), is one of those which make us draw our breath with wonder, and marvel as to whether it can properly bear the date attached to it (1814), so full is it of apparently matured knowledge and power. Only three pigs sleeping certainly, but what pigs they are, and how thoroughly asleep! Drawn, too, in such difficult positions, foreshortened with success, and together making a composition original and beautiful. Nor should we omit to note that the outside pigs by themselves fail to balance one another, the little piggy on the left being too small to make up its part of the proportion; but the boy, with what must have been an instinctive sense of harmony, has supplied the little one's deficiency by introducing a few

---

* *Art Journal*, May, 1875.

† In this year he produced his first portrait, at least the first that has been engraved, viz. "C. Simmons, Esq., on a Pony," engraved by C. Turner, A.R.A., in 1826.

A Cry of Distress (1814).

Drawn by Edwin Landseer aged 12 Years 1814

Merino Sheep (1814).

Plate IV.

strokes of a wooden railing, which cleverly adjusts the scale. A similar instance of happy adjustment will be found in the introduction of the broom in PLATE II., " A Short-horn Bull."

Belonging also to this year (1814), one in which he evidently made much progress, are the four drawings on PLATES III. and IV. As relating to the subjects just treated, it will be well first to call attention to " A Cry of Distress " (PLATE IV.), in which we have a man in the act of ringing a pig. The man is evidently a pork-butcher from the steel by his side, and is proceeding with his task in a very business-like manner. Though by no means equal to the pig, this figure is very much in advance of that in Fig. 15, especially in the action and drawing of the arms. A likeness is traceable between the two men, both in features and expression. Though very unfinished,

FIG. 17.—FARM-CARTS (1815).

there is great power in the pig, whose frantic endeavours to withdraw are given to the life, the "cry of distress" is almost audible, while the hindquarters and tail are by themselves quite tragic. He may indeed have been said to have thoroughly mastered all pig difficulties in this year, in which he produced a pair of pictures called respectively " A French Hog " and "A British Boar:" the former lean, long-legged, and gaunt as a wolf; the other as fat and round and short-legged as even a British pig could be and yet stand upright. These were so successful that he repeated them twice with slight alterations. All six were separately etched by Thomas Landseer.

The other drawing on the same page represents five merino sheep, which are said to have been "the first imported into this country by the late Lord Somerville, who exhibited them at the cattle show in 1814, at the Old Sadler's Repository, Goswell Road. Young Landseer presented the original drawing to Mrs. Sadler, in acknowledgment of her kind-

F

ness and attention during the five days he was sketching various animals ' on show.' In the distance is seen a spire, which, we are told, is that of Islington Church, then recently erected."* There is in the British Museum an etching by Thomas Landseer, after Edwin, of five sheep, of which three are identical in attitude and composition with those in our woodcut. These are the three to the left; but the two others are rams with twisted horns, separated from the left group and from each other, and are both lying down. The scene also is different, being a field with a hedge running across the plate behind the animals. Mr. Graves, in his catalogue, mentions a plate which is probably this, as etched by Thomas Landseer in 1818, from a drawing made by Edwin in 1813, and states that the sheep belonged to Squire Western. If the information in the *Art Journal* be correct, none of the sheep drawn in 1813, and belonging to Squire Western, could have been identical with any of those in our drawing, or the date given by Mr. Graves must be incorrect; but if they were a different lot it is singular that three of the sheep in each drawing should be so similar.

The animals on PLATE III. (1814) are specially interesting, as favourites of the young artist, who used to ride the pony and caress the dog. They belonged to Mr. George Wilson, uncle to the present possessor of the drawings, at whose residence at Walthamstow Landseer is said to have been a frequent visitor when a boy. They are both carefully done, but the dog is by far the better. His studies in anatomy have been of some value, and here for the first time we have a whole live standing dog, with every joint and muscle well defined, and the body as completely understood. The body looks somewhat ridgy and overworked, which may possibly be the effect of replacing his soft pencilling by the hard lines of a woodcut, but the labour is victorious, and such ill-made animals as Figs. 8 and 11 will never come from his pencil again. The next dog we give, drawn the next year, is a masterpiece.

This dog is "Brutus," PLATE V. (1815), a fine bull-terrier and a famous rat killer, which belonged to his early friend, Mr. W. W. Simpson, of Beleigh Grange, Essex, and was the father of another Brutus which belonged to Landseer himself when a boy. The first Brutus was often drawn by young Edwin. In Mr. Graves's catalogue two pictures of this dog are entered under the year 1815 (the same year as our drawing), one done for the top of a snuff-box, which is only a head, and another with a chestnut horse. Under the year 1817, in the same catalogue, we find a drawing of Old Brutus and a retriever, and in the Royal Academy catalogue of that year there is a portrait of Brutus. This, Mr. Graves thinks, was the head of Brutus exhibited at the Landseer Exhibition in 1874; and Mr. Stephens mentions another portrait of Brutus, whether the son or father is not quite clear, which was painted for Mr. Simpson in 1818, and represents "a white dog lying at the full length of his chain, with a

red earthenware dish." This year (1818) also produced a drawing of "Brutus with Two Dead Rats." We think it probable that all these were studies of the same dog, and that Brutus the younger was not immortalised till the year 1821, when he appeared with two other dogs, Boxer and Vixen, all belonging to the artist, in the well-known picture of the "Ratcatchers:" a subject which he repeated several times. This little catalogue of pictures of the elder Brutus is probably not exhaustive, but it shows how great a study of him Landseer made, and accounts for the great success of the drawing from which the woodcut on PLATE V. is taken. The drawing shows not only mastery of draughtsmanship but also of material, for it is outlined in pencil and worked up with black and white chalk. Here is no uncertainty about where each muscle should come : the dog stands firm on his four feet with a consensus of all parts

FIG. 18.—SUSPICIOUS (1815).

of the body, which shows the animal to have been comprehended as a whole as well as in detail. Nor is this all, for the artist's mind, being sure of the mechanical part, is able to spend its power upon character, and with the least possible work to give not only his body but his soul. Though, as we have seen, he mastered other animals before the dog, his mastery is now as complete over him as over any other animal.

How great that mastery was over the cow is shown by the group under "Brutus" on PLATE V., called "The Attack," where a bulldog has fastened on the throat of the poor beast, and means to hang there till further notice. His sport is, however, likely to be spoiled by the bull in the distance, who is galloping to the rescue with lumbering speed. This sketch, slight and early as it is, may well be reckoned among Landseer's masterpieces ; at no time of his life could he have improved upon it in vigour or expression.

This year (1815) is shown, by the specimens of his work in it which we give, to have been one of most careful study and of great progress. He had, at the end of the year, mastered all the domestic and farm animals-with the exception of the horse, and that he had nearly achieved a conquest over the difficulties of this animal is shown by his careful study of "A Cart Horse," which will be found in the chapter in this book specially devoted to his treatment of this animal. If we can set down the group in PLATE VI. to this year, he had undoubtedly mastered even the horse; but we think that this must be considered a later work. In addition to this he had begun to pay some attention to landscape and other objects which might be necessary as backgrounds to his figures or to be introduced into his pictures. This is obvious, not only in some of the backgrounds themselves, but also in Fig. 17—a careful study of "Farm Carts" and broken ground remarkable for its clever composition.

Down to this year (1815) all his instruction had been derived from his own study, aided by his father and perhaps his brothers, one of whom at least—Thomas—must have been of use to him in the technical part of etching; but in this year his father took him to Haydon, who gave him his dissections of the lion, and bid him dissect animals and study the Elgin Marbles, both of which precepts Edwin followed; but how much farther Haydon instructed him history does not say. Yet it was in 1815 that Landseer first exhibited in the Royal Academy. Nor, judging from the samples of his work at this period, can we be surprised that his contributions were not rejected. These were "Portrait of a Mule" and "Heads of a Pointer Bitch and Puppy," both the property of W. W. Simpson, Esq., of Beleigh Grange, Essex. The latter was exquisitely engraved by his brother Thomas three years later (1818). We do not know where Mr. Stephens obtained his information that Landseer was among the *honorary* exhibitors of the year, as in our copy of the Royal Academy Catalogue for 1815 he is included in the index of ordinary exhibitors as "Landseer, Master E., at Mr. Land-seer's, 33, Foley Street." In the same exhibition also appeared his portrait, done by a young friend who afterwards rose to some note as a portrait painter.[*] It is No. 450, and called "The Cricketer: a Portrait of Master E. Landseer. *Master J. Hayter.*" The account of Landseer's achievements this year would be incomplete without a notice of his magnificent drawing of an Alpine mastiff, which makes us sceptical as to the correctness of the date ascribed to one of the drawings we are about to mention.

We now come to two studies of dogs (Figs. 18 and 19) one called "Suspicious" and the other the "Dustman's Dog," which show that Landseer was gradually increasing his range of sentiment as well as of skill. In the first he has drawn a dog animated throughout with a feeling characteristic of many dogs, viz., suspicion.[†]

[*] Stephens, p. 38.
[†] The attitude and expression are very much like those of two bulls which he drew in 1811, who are evidently also on the *qui vive.*

On the Common (1815–18).

Plate VI.

Some sound or smell or sight has aroused in him a feeling that something or some-body wants looking after, and he is proceeding to look after him or her or it accordingly. With every sense alive, and with cat-like caution in his feet, he is approaching the neigh-bourhood of his distrust, and, unless the matter is cleared up to his perfect satisfaction, consequences are likely to ensue not altogether pleasant to the object of his inquiry. What sort of dog he is we confess ourselves unable to say; but it is not, at all events, a sort with which we should like to have a question even as to ancestry, and we would rather admit that he was a mastiff at once than dispute the point. But for the date affixed, the comparative weakness of the action in the hind legs, the anxiety after finish, and the unsatisfactory drawing of the feet would, without comparison with the Alpine mastiff before mentioned, incline us to refer this work to an earlier year.

The other study is dated 1816, and is the first we know in which he drew a dog

FIG. 19.—THE DUSTMAN'S DOG (1816).

whose character was affected by his master or his master's calling. The sympathy which so curiously exists between a man and his dog was a constant motive of Land-seer's work. This is the first, we may say, of a series of such studies which extended through a great part of his life. It is characteristic that he began very low down in the social scale; for he always showed much sympathy with the pariahs of brute society, at least in early life, and this is one. There is great pathos in this figure of the poor, tired, ill-favoured, unconsidered animal, with no claim to birth, accomplishments, or good looks, and quite unaccustomed to delicate fare or good society. His is a hard and humble life, and he seems to know it. To trudge after his master on his daily rounds, and to dine off the bones he can rake out of the rubbish heaps, this is all he can and does expect, considering himself fortunate when, as on the present occasion, he can find a bit of rug to lie upon while he sleeps with one eye open to watch his master's

G

bell. In this year (1816) he entered the schools of the Royal Academy, and it is not often that that institution admits a student who has so little to learn which the Academy could teach him.

Much, however, he had to learn from his own experience and the growth of his mind, and there is scarcely a drawing of this series which does not chronicle some advance in skill or increase in range of subject. Our next drawing of dogs, " The Braggart " (PLATE VII.), shows his first attempt at tracing the analogy between human and brute character, as the lion in Fig. 3 his first attempt at tracing similarity in appearance. This is also his first attempt at contrast of expression in the same composition, though the same current of thought is seen in the two pictures of the " French Hog " and " British Boar," to which we have before alluded. One notable point in this and the pictures of swine is the peculiar description of humour, which may be called Hogarthian in its endeavour to typify national character in a satirical manner. Indeed, in some respects, Landseer, though a painter of animals, more nearly approaches the spirit of Hogarth than any English painter. The picture for which this is a sketch was exhibited at the British Institution in the year 1820, and was called " The Three Dogs of England, Scotland, and Ireland ; from a Poem written by Thomas Bridgman, Esq., in imitation of Burns's ' Twa Dogs.' " The different characters and feelings of the three dogs, both in face and attitude, are wonderfully clever, and they tell their tale with very little overstepping of the limits of expressiveness allowed by nature to dumb animals.

Fig. 20, " Donkeys " (1810), may be usefully compared with the " Study of Donkeys " (1818) on PLATE VII.[*] It is difficult to say which is the more wonderful work, the first for a boy of eight, or the second for a boy of sixteen ; and yet what progress has been made in the eight years ! The first is a very careful drawing in pencil, with much character and truth of attitude ; but the donkeys are altogether too heavy, too thick in the neck, too massive in the jaws, too blunt in the ears ; but there is no defect, that we at least can discover, in the drawing of the beautiful group in PLATE VII. Sketched with the pen, and shaded with washes of sepia, we have the utmost truth obtainable by the means and amount of work employed, both with respect to character, drawing, and light and shade. Having regard to the beauty and variety of attitude, the cleverness of the grouping, and the mastery of execution, it is undoubtedly the most perfect, as it is the most beautiful, of the drawings which illustrate this chapter.

In some of these qualities it is, however, equalled, if not surpassed, by PLATE VI., called " On the Common," but which is evidently intended as a family study of horse,

---

[*] And both of them with a most spirited etching of " Donkeys and Foal " (1811), of which there is a copy in the British Museum.

THE BRAGGART (1818).

E L. 1818

STUDY OF DONKEYS (1818).

PLATE VII.

donkey, and mule. Smallest of all, the jackass stands on the right; on the left the mother mare towers above her offspring and its father; behind, but not so hidden by its parents that its hybrid peculiarities are not visible, stands the mule. As a triumph over the difficulties of foreshortening, the ass and mare are more wonderful than anything we have yet shown of Landseer's work, and in skill in obtaining the utmost possible result for the minimum of labour it will bear comparison with the work of any artist of any time. If this was done in the latest year of the three affixed to it (1815-18), it shows that at the age of sixteen he was already without any living rival in the art of drawing animals, except James Ward, R.A.; and it shows, what is more to the purpose of this chapter, that he had added the horse to the list of the animals the difficulties of drawing which he had thoroughly mastered.

To sum up the results of this chapter, between the ages of five and sixteen Landseer learnt how to draw perfectly pigs, cattle, dogs (at least, short-haired dogs), cats, donkeys, and probably sheep and lions. He could draw in pencil, chalk, ink, and sepia, and combine them with perfect mastery. He could etch very well and paint in oils. He had attained considerable skill in composition, and could animate his animals with the character belonging to their kind, with individual character, and, in the case of dogs, with semi-human character and expression. He could take portraits, and had studied the human figure, and he had shown that he possessed pathetic, humorous, and satirical power

Fig. 20.—Donkeys (1810—11).

FIG. 21.—TIRED (1820).

CHAPTER II.

1818—24.

THE first chapter brings the artistic biography of Landseer down to the time when, though only sixteen years old, he had mastered most of the technical difficulties of his profession, and was an accomplished artist in the workman sense of the term. He had, however, always been something more; the desire to reach the spirit and essence of his subject being observable in his earliest drawings, and his imagination only waited till his hand was equal in skill to express its conceptions. The description of his mental powers had also been in a great measure shown. as we have already seen; so that on reviewing his work from first to last we scarcely come upon any new faculty after his sixteenth year, although the manner in which his genius developed, and the results it produced, were more striking and various than could possibly have been predicted.

But at present (1818) the power being proved, and the skill attained, the question was, "What will he do with them?" A question this which probably caused the artist a good deal of thinking, and which, as such questions generally are, was resolved, for the most part, by circumstances. We have seen that he never had any doubt about what the principal subjects of his art were to be: animals, and their associations. It only remained to discover what animals he was to paint, and in what spirit he was to treat them. In this respect also he appears to have been freer from doubt than most artists, and to have made no false starts; but that he was not altogether certain of his chief strength is obvious from the tentative efforts he made in various directions before he struck out the path which was to lead to his unexampled fame; and if he made no false start, there was at least one ambition in art which, after a little while, was, to a great extent, relinquished, viz. what may be called the treatment of animals as materials for compositions in which grandeur of design and robust action were the

FIG. 22.—RESTING (1818).

chief aims. But he did not relinquish these for want of power or from failure in execution, but because they were less in accordance with the spirit of himself and his time, and because success in other directions was sure and easy.

But whatever dreams or intentions the youth of sixteen may have had with regard to the future of his art (and here we may mention that there appear to be no published data from which any notion of the inner life of the artist, now or afterwards, can be derived), there was one great obstacle to the fulfilling of them, viz. that his education as a painter of pictures was unfinished. Wonderful as was the skill he had attained in drawing animals, he was comparatively a beginner in the representation of those various scenes in which his *dramatis personæ* were to play their parts. His knowledge

of landscape was very limited, and his drawings of human figures were not up to the
mark required. The little sketch of " Resting," 1818 (Fig. 22), shows, indeed, great
care, especially in the drawing of the plants ; but it is obvious that it is the work of a
prentice hand, and that it would form a very weak background for one of his most
carelessly executed animals of this period. This same weakness is shown in the background to the drawing of " An Impending Quarrel " (Fig. 23), where the dog and cat,
though by no means so good as some of his animals already given, are spirited, and
are little, if at all, aided by the barn and landscape behind. In " A Pigsty" (Fig. 24),
and " Milking-time " (Fig. 25), the background is nothing but a few lines to represent

FIG. 23.—AN IMPENDING QUARREL (1818).

the interior of a sty and shed respectively, while in the next, " The Donkey-ride "
(Fig. 26), the landscape is of the most elementary kind. In the drawing of a deer
which heads this chapter (Fig. 21) the landscape is so " conspicuous by its absence "
that a writer in the *Art Journal* has been fain to suggest that the animal is leaping
over a chasm. In 1822 he obtained the assistance of Mr. Patrick Nasmyth to paint the
background of the " Bull and the Frog ;" and as late as the year 1824 the artist appears
to have been conscious of his comparative shortcomings in this respect, for after he had
painted Lion, the Alpine mastiff, which he had drawn perfectly in 1815, or nine years before,
he asked its owner, Mr. W. H. de Merle, to allow him to defer painting the background

until he had paid his first visit to Scotland.* For these reasons the period between 1818 and 1825, or the year after his first visit to Scotland, is necessarily a period in which he had to turn his attention so much to study as to be unable to give rein to his creative power except in certain limited directions.

But his conquests over animal drawing enabled him to achieve considerable success as a painter even in this year (1818) by a picture called " Fighting Dogs getting Wind," which was exhibited at the Society of Painters in Oils and Watercolours. It considerably added to his reputation, made by his picture of " A Sleeping Dog," a mastiff, exhibited in their room the preceding year. A very enthusiastic notice of the " Fighting Dogs " is quoted by Mr. Stephens from the *Examiner* of 1818, in which the critic writes, " Did we only see the dog's collar, we should know it was produced by

FIG. 24.—A PIGSTY (1818).

no common hand, so good is it and palpably true. But the gasping, and cavernous, and redly-stained mouths, the flaming eyes, the prostrate dog, and his antagonist standing exultingly over him, the inveterate rage that superior strength inflames but cannot subdue, with the broad and bright relief of the objects, give a wonder-producing vitality to the canvas."† Making some allowance for the writer's enthusiasm, this was evidently a masterly work, remarkable for vigour and truth, and one of a class which is only found in his earlier pictures. " An Impending Quarrel," 1818 (Fig. 23), in which violent action is only imminent, and the spirit of which is humorous rather than passionate, is more characteristic of the painter's work viewed as a whole. According

* Graves, p. 9, No. 80.   † Stephens, p. 55.

to the *Art Journal,*[*] this is Brutus, but whether the first or second of that name [†] is not certain. In appearance and attitude it is not unlike the picture of 1824, which was Brutus the younger, the artist's own dog, an engraving from which, by Thomas Landseer, appeared in the *Annals of Sporting.* In the 1824 picture the scene is the interior of a stable, and the object of Brutus's attention is an exceedingly evil-looking bulldog, whose head appears through the aperture between the nearly closed door and the side of the stable. If it were not for the chain, which prevents the door from opening

FIG. 25.—MILKING-TIME (1818).

more widely, the "impending quarrel" in this case would be much more serious than that in our woodcut.

Still farther removed from violent action is the clever drawing of "A Pigsty" (Fig. 24), and it only needs a remark here as the last example we have to give of a simple study by the artist of farm-animals, made without any definite intention except practice or pleasure. This may be said to end the series of such studies, in which this collection is so rich; studies which, though they all show cleverness not only of drawing but design, were not meant to be worked up into pictures, but were an end to themselves. In the next we give our last of such studies of farm labourers—"Milking-time" (Fig. 25)—showing great care in study of the attitude of the milker and the folds

---

of his smock. If we compare this drawing with the well-known picture of "The Maid and the Magpie," we shall see so much difference in so many things that it will appear waste of time to consider the two together; but there is one essential difference between the two which it is worth our while to mention here, and that is, that in the early sketch the human figure was introduced as an appanage to the cow, in the other the cow is an appanage to the human figure. The one shows the commencement of Landseer's love of animals, the latter its conclusion. He first loved them for themselves, and only cared for men (artistically) in so far as they were necessary to illustrate their lives and habits. As he grew older, and became a man himself, and mixed with men, he began

FIG. 26.—THE DONKEY-RIDE (1818).

to look upon animals more and more in relation to men, until at the end animals had little interest for him except in such relation. If he drew a dog it was as the servant of man, or as a pet of a man, and to convey some human sentiment; if he drew stags it was as a sportsman or a poet. There are some, we believe, who think that this was wrong—that he should have devoted his powers to showing us what animals were in themselves, and what life was to them, instead of their human suggestiveness; and we think that in some of his most playful works he subordinated animal truth to human pleasure of a not sufficiently serious kind; but there was nothing ignoble even in his most playful work, and in his highest the human sentiment not only

1

dignifies the pictures with a noble poetry, which far exceeds in value any loss of purely animal spirit, but dignifies the animals themselves by extending their influence for good and for pleasure beyond the limits assigned to their sphere of intelligence.

Landseer was of far too kindly a nature ever to take pleasure in the sufferings of animals, and we very seldom find him even making pictorial fun out of their misfortunes, but instances of this do now and then occur, and one of them is "The Donkey-ride" (Fig. 26), where a boy is riding a tethered donkey, and is urging it forward with a stick, while a dog behind barks at the poor brute's heels.   This drawing

FIG. 27.—ON THE SCENT (1819).

is, in the motive of its humour, something like one of Landseer's etchings called "The Sweeps," belonging to the year 1822, in which a poor, broken-kneed, bareboned scarecrow of a horse is bestrided by two sweeps and a seedy-looking youth, the latter riding on the haunches of the animal with his face to the tail, while before the overladen screw there limps a small dog with a ludicrous gait as if in imitation of the horse.   In this year he exhibited a picture of a donkey at the Royal Academy which was praised by Wilkie in a letter to Haydon.*

* Stephens, p. 55.

Next we come to two studies of sporting dogs, both intended for setters we presume, but "On the Scent" (Fig. 27) looks like a cross between a pointer and setter, with a good deal of its hair rubbed off. It is evidently very unfinished, but shows great spirit and character in the eagerness of its attitude and the way in which its long supple body accommodates itself to the unevenness of the ground; the other—"Setter Dogs" (Fig. 28)—is a very slight but clever sketch. These dogs look more like spaniels than setters. This year seems to have been principally devoted to studies of dogs, all the works of it chronicled in Mr. Graves's catalogues being pictures of these animals or compositions containing them. One of his pictures exhibited at the British Institution this year was a "Newfoundland Dog and Rabbit," in which the

FIG. 28.—SETTER DOGS (1819).

dog is fine and the rabbit perhaps finer. It was sold at Christie's in July, 1877, for £388 10s., and belonged to Mr. Dymoke, the Hereditary Champion.

Next year was exhibited at the same gallery the "Braggart," of which we give the original sketch (PLATE VII.), and also "Alpine Mastiffs reanimating a Distressed Traveller," a picture which made a great sensation, and which still, by means of the engraving by his father, John Landseer, assisted by Thomas, retains its popularity. Of this picture we also give the original sketch (Fig. 30)—a very rough one—in which one dog is put in and the position of the other indicated. This picture was the result of the artist's studies from Alpine mastiffs, of which the extent is shown by his pictures of those animals. One called "Lion," and belonging to a

Mr. Boodly or Bullock, was drawn in 1815 and exhibited at the Society of Painters in Oil and Watercolours in 1817, and "A Sleeping Mastiff" was exhibited at the British Institution in 1818. In the picture of 1820 the animal to the left is Cæsar, the son of Mr. Bullock's Lion. In 1824 he drew Mr. W. H. de Merle's Lion, of which mention has already been made.* The picture of 1820 is very interesting as showing how cleverly he managed to get over the difficulties of the landscape, when he had a good subject which called upon him to exert his imagination and ingenuity. Certainly

FIG. 29.—DENIZENS OF THE ROCKS (1820).

at this time he had never seen mountains, and yet he was able to conceive and execute on a large scale a background of an Alpine scene in winter, and one effective in design and sufficiently truthful to serve its purpose. When one remembers that four years later he would not paint in a background to a portrait of one of the same dogs until he had been to Scotland, one wonders at the temerity of youth, and the triumph of determination over difficulties which is one of the true signs of genius.

On PLATE VIII. will be found two drawings of the same year (1820), which afford a

---

* Page 26.

THE END OF ALL LABOUR (1820).

WAKING UP (1820).

PLATE VIII.

contrast which might be made the subject of a sermon; the lusty, violent, bloodthirsty lion waking up refreshed and hungering after some new prey, and the poor harmless overworked horse who will never wake again. But the contrast which concerns us most is that between the spirits of the two styles: the one pathetic, realistic; the other violent and imaginative. The first was simply a study made in a knacker's yard—an unusual sort of study, but still nothing more nor less than one instigated by his usual feeling for animals and his habits of industry; the other the result of his early boyish semi-romantic dreams of lions, and the precepts of Haydon about "high art," and perhaps ambition to rank with Rubens and Snyders, all stimulated anew by a recent incident —the death of one of the lions at Exeter Change—which enabled him to make fresh studies from dissection of a real specimen. In this year he exhibited two very large canvases at the British Institution, one, eight feet by six, "A Lion disturbed at his Repast," and the other "A Lion enjoying his Repast"—and next year "A Prowling Lion" at the Royal Academy, for one or other of which this was probably a study. That the spirit of "high art" was upon him is evident, moreover, from the fact that he turned this drawing of the horse in the knacker's yard (or rather a replica of it) into a "composition," by adding a landscape and calling it "The Vulture's Prey." This was etched by Mr. C. G. Lewis for Mr. Hogarth, to whom the drawing belonged; but Mr. Lewis asked for and obtained the drawing as payment for the plate. Fine as both these drawings certainly are, we should value the dead cart-horse above the living lion. Whether the drawing "Denizens of the Rocks" (Fig. 29) was made in connection with the "Vulture's Prey" we do not know; but it is interesting as having been made in the same year, and for its being the first drawing of birds by Landseer of which we have any record, except a parrot in the South Kensington Museum.

Belonging to the same year, and showing the same kind of ambition, is the fine "Bull attacked by Dogs" (PLATE IX.), a drawing which it is somewhat remarkable that he did not utilise as the subject of a picture. A part of the composition, however, he did use, not only once, but twice, as any one can see who takes the trouble to compare it with the still finer "Contending Group after Nature," engraved by Thomas Landseer for a work called "Twenty-six Engravings of Lions, Tigers," &c., to which we have previously called attention,* and of which a republication was issued some years after by Mr. H. Bohn, accompanied by Landseer's illustrations to the "Annals of Sporting." In this group a lion takes the place of the bull, a leopard that of the dog under the belly of the bull, and a tiger on his back that of the dog in front. A similar arrangement will also be found in the picture of "Chevy Chase," the bull being replaced by a stag.

The year 1820 is also remarkable for his first studies of an animal from which he was to draw inspiration for some of his most beautiful and noble pictures. Though he

---

* Page 5.

K

could scarcely have had an opportunity of seeing red deer in their natural state, or even of seeing one hunted in England, these first drawings (Figs. 21 and 32) show a great feeling for the animal, and must have been the result of study. The sketches of eyes in the corner of Fig. 21, and sketches of other parts of the animal in the possession of Mr. C. G. Lewis, attest the study.

The two drawings of "Vixen" (PLATE X.) are assigned to the years 1821 and 1824. Vixen, Brutus, and Boxer were Landseer's three dogs, and were painted together in a picture called the "Ratcatchers," exhibited at the Royal Academy in 1821.[*] In

FIG. 30.—ALPINE MASTIFFS (1820).

our eyes the "Vixen" stated to belong to 1824 is so far better drawn as to justify the later date, but we are puzzled by a date on the drawing itself which looks like 1816. Vixen was a thoroughbred Scotch terrier and a famous ratter.

In 1822 he executed his first lithograph from a picture of a Labrador bitch exhibited in the British Institution in that year and called " A Watchful Sentinel." Of this picture we give the sketch in our chapter on dogs.[†] He also continued his compositions from

---

[*] There were three or four pictures of this name exhibited at different exhibitions in various years.

[†] Fig. 88, "Com."

BULL ATTACKED BY DOGS (1821).

beasts of prey in a series of six very fine drawings, engraved by Thomas Landseer, and published in the work lately alluded to as containing the "Contending Group after Nature." One of these—a lion with his paw on a sceptre and a background of rock, which forms the "engraved title" of the volume—has a calmness and fulness of dignity scarcely surpassed by his noble sculptures on the Nelson Monument. In this year he also began the series of seventeen etchings which were collected and published afterwards. The first of these is the "Dogs worrying a Frog," and the next "The Ladies' Pets"—a pug dog and a spaniel, of exceeding fatness, toiling after their mistresses on a hot day. In the next year (1824) he added three to the series—"A Shepherd's Dog," "The Beggar," and "Donkeys and Horses"—all of which are excellent in their different ways, but all showing the deficiency in landscape to which we have before alluded. This, when he had visited Scotland the year after, was amply supplied by the lovely "Travellers' Rest," "The Spring," and "The Mountain Torrent," to say nothing of the landscapes to the other etchings of this year—"The Eagle and Dead Red Deer" and "The Watchman."

But the careful way in which he studied landscape, and the high degree of skill he had reached in 1824, especially in the drawing of leafage and herbage, are shown in the two drawings in PLATE XXXI., the original of one of which, "The Angler's Guard," is in the Sheepshanks collection, and is almost as brilliant and minute in touch as a miniature on ivory; but the touch is what Wilkie complained of as "niggling," and the colour crude. He was apparently spoiling his early pictures, as he did some of his early drawings, by over, or rather wrong, finish. But during these six years he had done a great deal of work, shown a wonderful facility for design, and achieved success in everything he attempted. And there was a stamp upon even his slightest study which distinguished it as essentially greater in conception than the work of other men. The chief classes of work at this time may be said to have been (1) the grand style of animal painting in emulation of the old masters, to which belong his fine compositions and studies of the carnivora; (2) humorous composition, which may be subdivided into the humours of animals and humorous aspects of animals—to the first belong such as "Dogs worrying a Frog" and "An Impending Quarrel" (Fig. 23), to the latter such as "A Donkey-ride" (Fig. 26) and "The Ladies' Pets;" (3) pathetic compositions, such as "The Vulture's Prey"—see "The End of all Labour" (1820), PLATE VIII.—and the study of the harried deer (Figs. 21 and 32); (4) studies of animal character and habits, wild and trained, such as the "Ratcatchers," the various sporting dogs, the "Alpine Mastiff reanimating a Dead Traveller" (Fig. 30), and the "Hare and Foxes" (PLATE XXX.).

His greatest successes in exhibited pictures during these years were—if we may judge from the popularity of engravings—the "Alpine Mastiffs" (1820), the "Ratcatchers" (1821), the "Larder Invaded" (1822)—which obtained a premium from the British Institution of £150—and the "Cat's Paw" (1824), the last of which is perhaps now the most generally known. The sketch from which our woodcut (Fig. 31) of this subject is taken differs in several respects from the picture which was exhibited at the British Institution in 1824, and now in the possession of the Earl of Essex, who bought it for £120. In the picture the monkey is on a rush-bottomed chair, and has got the cat into a more comfortable position (for himself). She is well up under his arm, and her face, with its impotent rage, comes out in

FIG. 31.—THE CAT'S PAW (1824).

better contrast against the cunning and cruel profile of the monkey, whose face is less humorous and more ruthless and determined than in the sketch. He has also guarded himself better against the attacks of the cat, both by a cloth in which she is wrapped and the position in which he holds her. In the picture one of her feet is digging its claws into her own flank instead of the monkey's back. The chafing-dish is replaced by a stove, which is somewhat higher and more convenient for the monkey, while the agony and sense of sound is increased by the presence of two kittens, one in a

Vixen (1821).

Vixen (1824).

Plate X.

clothes-basket and one out, who bewail their mother's predicament with unavailing cries. An upset coalscuttle, a broken dish, and scattered clothes, show that the triumph of the monkey has not been attained without a fearful preliminary scrimmage.

To this year belong his first illustration, "Sancho Panza and Dapple," now at South Kensington, and his first portrait-group, "The Bedford Family."

FIG. 32.—THE CHASE (1820).

L

FIG. 33.—SIR WALTER SCOTT (1831).

CHAPTER III.

1824—1834.

THE year of 1824 is to be specially marked in the history of Landseer's art as that in which he went to Scotland with Sir Walter Scott. This event, which would be an important one in any person's history, had for his art effects which amounted to little less than a regeneration. Fond of nature and animals as he always was, that fondness became now a more living and concentrated force under the influence of wild and romantic scenery and the characteristic beauty of its animals. To the latter alone belongs a poetry of form and character which breathes a completely different spirit to any to be found in association with the southern country. The Grampians are not more opposite to Salisbury Plain, in the ideas which they inspire, than a deerhound to a foxhound, a blackcock to a partridge, a collie to an English shepherd's dog, or a red to a fallow deer. To a mind like that of Landseer, which had always the strongest sympathy with whatever was great or noble or refined, the introduction to Scotland must have been like the fulfilment of an ideal, especially under the auspices of a man like Sir Walter Scott, who, now in the zenith of his fame and before the blight of pecuniary difficulties had come upon him (before even the shadow of them had been seen in the distance), must have been the man of all others to stimulate and direct his imagination. What personal influence the great novelist and poet had upon Sir Edwin we do not know, except from his art, which certainly partook something of his spirit from this time, as is shown in his studies of hawking and pictures of "the olden time," to say nothing of his illustrations to the Waverley Novels, in which he caught the feeling not only of the animals but of the human characters as well. His "David Gellatley" ("Waverley") is little inferior in spirit to "Ban and Buscar," and his "Edie Ochiltree" ("Antiquary") almost as fine in its way as "Bevis" ("Woodstock"). To Scott's influence may also be safely ascribed the picture of "Chevy Chase" painted in 1826, as well as the sketch from the "Lady of the Lake" (Fig. 37) and that of "Friar Tuck" (Fig. 77).

We therefore think ourselves justified in heading this chapter with the rough, but

FIG. 34.—MAIDA (1827).

thoroughly conceived, sketches of the head of Sir Walter in Fig. 33, although they were not executed till seven years after the commencement of the period of which this chapter treats. Nor do we think any apology is needed for presenting the portrait of "Maida" (Fig. 34) in close companionship with his loving master, who himself, though with different means, drew so noble a portrait of him in his novel of "Woodstock" under the name of Bevis. When Landseer went to Abbotsford poor Maida was very near his end. On the 22nd of October, 1824, Sir Walter wrote to his second son, Charles, (then at Brasenose College, Oxford), "I have a little domestic news to tell you. Old Maida died quietly in his straw last week, after a good supper, which, considering his weak state, was rather a deliverance." The year (1827) under our woodcut is that in which Landseer painted "A Scene at Abbotsford," in which Maida is introduced "in

the last stage of weakness and debility, as the artist has admirably expressed in his
fading eyes and attenuated limbs.   He died six weeks afterwards."*   We therefore
think that there is good ground for believing that the sketch we engrave was taken in
1824, during Landseer's visit to Abbotsford in that year.   In 1832 Landseer drew a
portrait of "Bevis" for "Woodstock," which is said to represent Maida; but if so it is
Maida in the height of his strength and beauty, as imagined by the artist.   The deer-
hound in "High Life," of a sketch of which we give a woodcut in our chapter on
dogs, is also said to be a reminiscence of Maida; but the dog in the picture of "High

FIG. 35.—DEAD STAG (1824).

Life," now in the Vernon Gallery, is not of the same colour as Maida;† but as Maida
was the first staghound from which Landseer studied, he is the artistic father of
many such dogs, and probably in his sphere exercised little less influence over Landseer's art than his master did in his.   There is also a portrait of Maida exquisitely
etched by Sir Edwin and published in his series of etchings; the date of this is 1824.

The first sight of red deer in their native "forests" (so called apparently on the
principle of *lucus a non lucendo*) was also a revelation to Landseer.   Fond always of
sport, but more from his interest in animal life than from his delight in destruction,

---

* Graves, p. 11.   † Graves, p. 13.

there was a difference to him between deerstalking in the Highlands and English sports, of kind as well as of degree. For the first time his sympathies were strongly excited by the nobility and beauty of the animal to be slain. He went as a boy to bull-baitings and bear-baitings; but there is nothing in his drawings of these to show that he enjoyed the sport. He was naturally humane, and cared for them only as opportunities for the study of character, just as Thackeray went to see a man hanged. From the first his feeling in connection with sport was always manly and right. His

FIG. 36.—PONY AND DEAD DEER (1825).

drawings of rat-catching show a very proper sympathy with the courage and determination of terriers in the destruction of vermin, and those of English sporting dogs a delight in their beauty and sagacity. It is plain from his pictures in which the cat is the object of pursuit, that he saw the *dog's* fun thoroughly, but sympathized with poor pussy, whom he always put in a safe place. The only exception we know to the humanity of his art in connection with field sports is one of the Woburn game-lists, in which each division is headed with a little etching of an animal in the agonies of death:

M

the pheasant is tumbling down with the feathers flying from its neck, and the rabbit, just struck, is turning over on its side with one little forepaw raised in the most pathetic manner. These drawings seem to us to insist upon just the point in connection with all sport which is most painful, and which if dwelt upon by sportsmen would either put a stop to sport or make them delight in cruelty. We have no doubt that the artist's motive.

FIG. 37.—SCENE FROM "THE LADY OF THE LAKE" (1825—26).

though perhaps unconsciously, was sympathy with the unfortunate victims ; but it would not be a pleasant list to use. At any rate it is certain that he never derived any pleasure from cruelty, and this first drawing of a "Dead Stag" (Fig. 35), 1824, shows far more of the spirit of the artist than of the sportsman, being imbued with the greatest feeling for the beauty and dignity of the animal which has been destroyed.

The same feeling for the inherent majesty of the stag, whether alive or dead, is clearly shown in all his drawings of this animal, whether they are mere studies, as in Fig. 36, "Pony and Dead Deer," or in his most carefully-finished and poetical pictures, such as "Night" and "Morning." In our figure there is a pathetic helplessness in the grouping of the legs and a surviving dignity in the lifeless head, while the little sturdy pony on which it is bound seems to be aware of the royalty of its burden.

The influence both of Sir Walter Scott and of the deer is shown in our next sketch (Fig. 37), "Scene from 'The Lady of the Lake,'" which is remarkable for its spirit and design, and for being one of his earliest, if not his earliest, attempt at "illustration." The scene is from Canto I., and shows the "antlered monarch of the waste" at the end of his long chase, when, after having outrun all but two of the dogs and all but one of the riders, he is nearing

> "that mountain high,
> The lone lake's western boundary,"

where "the hunter"

> "deemed the stag must turn to bay."

The actual lines of which the sketch is the illustration are in the seventh stanza, and are too fine to leave unquoted :—

> "Alone, but with unbated zeal,
> That horseman plied the scourge and steel ;
> For jaded now, and spent with toil,
> Embossed with foam and dark with soil,
> While every gasp with sobs he drew,
> The labouring stag strained still in view.
> Two dogs of black St. Hubert's breed,
> Unmatched for courage, strength, and speed,
> Fast on his flying traces came
> And all but won that desperate game ;
> For scarce a spear's length from his haunch
> Vindictive toil'd the bloodhounds staunch ;
> Nor nearer might the dogs attain,
> Nor farther might the quarry strain.
> Thus up the margin of the lake,
> Between the precipice and brake,
> O'er stock and rock their race they take."

One of the dogs is evidently too much spent to continue the chase, which does not accord with the poem ; but it is a pity that Landseer never worked up the sketch into a picture, or made another attempt to illustrate this scene and others from Sir Walter's poems, where his sympathy with the author's spirit and the various moods of nature would have enabled him to exercise his imagination to advantage.

Another point of remark in this sketch is its excessive freedom and slightness.

These qualities are indeed such as one would expect in a drawing of an imaginary
scene; but from this time we find that not only imaginary but ordinary studies are
executed with a dash and carelessness the very reverse of the patient accuracy of
his former manner. Of this the "Highland Interior" (Fig. 38) is an example. A
similar change was soon observable in his painting, of which Mr. Stephens says
his "style of execution changed [in 1827] from sound and deliberate firmness of
youthful practice to the broader, freer, and more effective mode" which afterwards
characterized his workmanship.* With regard to his sketches, this change was no

FIG. 38.—HIGHLAND INTERIOR (1825).

doubt due to his consciousness of mastery and the different object with which he
made them. They were no longer an end in themselves, but material for future
pictures; no longer studies for the acquisition of technical skill and knowledge, but
memoranda jotted down in the quickest way for the assistance of his memory,
containing no more and no less than was necessary to preserve main facts and fix
impressions. It is necessary therefore that we on our part should also change our
point of view, and look upon his sketches less as steps in his artistic progress than as
materials for the pictures by which that progress was hereafter to be traced. His

* Stephens, p. 78.

A Deer-hound (1826).

A Dead Roe (1826).

Plate XI.

student life was, in the technical sense, over, and it is in the extension of the range over which his mind sought subjects for his art that his future development must be traced.

One direction into which he made resolute excursions, now necessarily for the first time, was the habits and character of the Highlanders. In the year 18:6 he exhibited at the British Institution a picture of an "Interior of a Highland Cottage;" in 1829, at the Royal Academy, "An Illicit Whiskey Still in the Highlands;" in 183:

FIG. 39.—A HIGHLAND CABIN.

an "Interior of a Highlander's House" and the "Poacher's Bothy" at the Royal Academy, and the "Highland Cradle" at the British Institution—all connected with the life of poor Highlanders—not to mention other pictures of the same class, such as "Too Hot" and "Highland Music." In this respect he also showed his sympathy with Sir Walter Scott, whose love of romance was not more marked than his interest in the daily life of the poor, who cared as much for the bothy as the castle, and for the collie as for the deer-hound. The link between these two great men is shown in the

N

"Fireside Party," painted in 1829, in which Landseer introduced dogs of the veritable breed of Pepper and Mustard, so well known to all lovers of "Guy Mannering." These are the first of Landseer's pictures in which the human element is of importance.

FIG. 40.—A HIGHLAND MAIDEN (1827).

The figures may be introduced for the sake of the dogs; but it is as the associates of men that the dogs have interest for the artist.

Two sketches of these Highland interiors are engraved in Figs. 38 and 39, the

THE HIGHLAND WHISKEY STILL (1827).

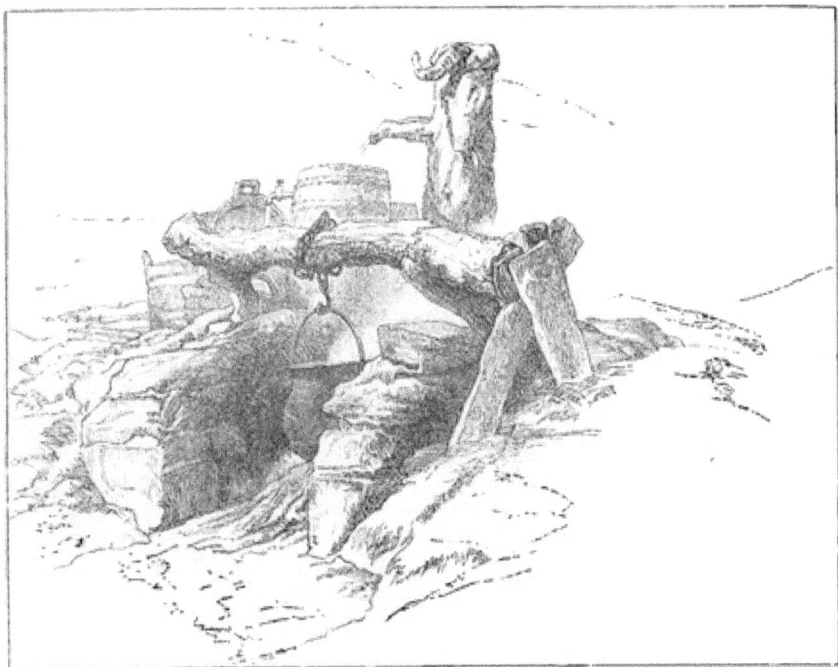

A WHISKEY STILL (1827).

PLATE XII.

former of which is dated Glen Errick, 1825, and is drawn in pencil with washes of tint—a favourite practice of Landseer. Our woodcut is only remarkable as a study of light and shade.

The other is supposed to have been suggested by a scene in "Redgauntlet." It is very masterly and the figures are full of character; but it is too unfinished to have any but artistic interest, even if the subject of it were identified.

The finest of all Landseer's pictures of Highland, indeed of human, character, is, we think, the "Illicit Whiskey Still in the Highlands;" of the studies for which we give

FIG. 41.—SCOTCH BEGGARS (1828).

three, the "Highland Maiden" (Fig. 40), 1827, and the two on PLATE XII. Though so slightly sketched, we prefer our Highland Maiden to that in the finished picture or that in the "Rustic Beauty"—a separate engraving of her figure published as a companion to "Beauty's Bath," the well-known portrait of Miss Eliza Peel with her dog Fido. This maiden in Fig. 40 is wilder and not so well clothed or combed as when she dressed herself for the picture, but she has more character and also a finer face; nor do we think that, for simplicity and originality of composition, Landseer ever did anything better than this rude sketch; but the proprietor of the still in the picture is a great improvement upon the ordinary looking Highlander in PLATE XII. (1827), who might be the most tame and law-loving of men, dressed in Highland costume and indulging in chemical experiments.   It is far different in the picture, where he is the incarnation of bold lawlessness—a man of hard life and strong passions, who is trying the new brew with a face critical for the moment—a man with an eye like an eagle and thews of whipcord, who might be a stanch friend, but would assuredly be a relentless enemy.   There is, however, a dare-devilry in his mien which inspires him with that touch of romance so dear to human nature, if exhibited even by robbers, and one cannot

FIG. 42.—SETTERS (1828).

help feeling that one would be sorry that he should be taken for cheating the excise. All three of these drawings are as masterly as they can well be, every touch performing the exact work required of it, and being full of meaning, whether its object be to express human, animal, or what is called " still " life. In the sketch on the top of PLATE XII. should be observed the first glimpse of Scotch scenery, with firs, which, though slightly touched, are wonderfully true and varied in growth ; also the exceeding cleverness with which the rough shed or arbour of boughs and heath is expressed, and the interior lighted, showing with great distinctness the illicit machinery.   Though only a sketch it has all the materials of a complete picture, so thoroughly one is it in conception, from the man and dog which form its central interest to the landscape behind which completes his isolation. " Completes his isolation " we say, because it is evident

Rent (1829—30).

Plate XIII.

from that uplifted hand, under which he is gazing into the distance, that the country in front of him is as wild and empty of human life as that we see behind. If, indeed, he see any figures approaching they are not likely to be any more civilised or disturbing to the illicit mind than the group of tattered fellow countrymen in Fig. 41 (1828).

More remarkable for its beautiful background of Scotch moorland than for the dog, which wants character and has (at least in our cut) something very much the matter with one of its forelegs, is the drawing of "A Deerhound" (1826) on PLATE XI. This sketch is in oils, which from this time he frequently employed for studies. Below it

FIG. 43.—HIGHLANDER AND PONY (1829).

is a cut from a fine drawing of a "Roedeer" in the same year, one of whose haunches has been cut off, the remains of which and a dirk are lying on the ground. It reminds one of the scene in Donald Bean's cavern in "Waverley," where the Highlanders, dropping in in the course of the night, proceeded to cut steaks off the carcases suspended in his *spence* and broil them over the coals; but Donald Bean is not stated to have had a roedeer in his larder on that occasion.

These years, so productive of sketches and so marked by a new impulse to his art, were not marked by any great success in the exhibitions, if we except the "Chevy Chase" of 1826, which appears to be the result of his old ambition to rival Snyders

o

mingling with his recently acquired romantic sentiment. The spirit of Haydon and the spirit of Scott were, however, too distinct to mix well, and the result, though in many respects a fine composition, can scarcely be reckoned among the successes of his life. He was elected an Associate of the Royal Academy in this year, when only twenty-four years old, *i.e.*, at the earliest age permitted by the rules of the Academy. In the next year (1827) he exhibited at the rooms of this society his well-known pictures of " The Monkey who had seen the World " and " The Deerstalker's Return," which have since sold for £1,575 and £1,680 respectively, and at the British Institution, " A Scene from Abbotsford " previously noticed. In 1828, the year to which "Setters " (Fig. 42) belongs, he exhibited nothing of importance ; but in a drawing of "A Dog howling on the Sea Coast " (or rather, we think, "the shores of a lake "), a woodcut of which was published in Nimrod's "Sporting," he first struck the deep note of pathos which vibrates most sadly and sweetly in "Suspense" and the "Shepherd's Chief Mourner." In this drawing, engraved by Hixon on wood, a dog is seated on his haunches on the margin of a lake or the sea, howling, with outstretched neck, for the loss of his master, whose " bonnet " and feather have just been washed to the dog's feet.

The year 1829—to which the very clever pen-and-ink sketch of a "Highlander and Pony " (Fig. 43) belongs—was marked by several pictures of importance, among which were the "Highland Whiskey Still" and the "Fireside Party" already mentioned, and the pair of "High Life " and "Low Life"—the value of which is not to be measured by their size, which is very small. " Low Life " was a reproduction in oils of his etching of 1822, one of the best fruits of his ante-Highland time ; " High Life " belonged distinctly to his post-Highland time ; and the contrast was one not only good in idea, but very honourable to the artist, showing as it did that the spirits of the two periods were equally good in their different ways, and that each could bear contrast with the other. As there was nothing vulgar in his early humour, so there was nothing ignoble in his later refinement. We cannot, however, think of the contrast without regret at the thought that the high life was henceforward to get so completely the better of it in Landseer's art. With the exception of the " Jack in Office," the celebrated picture of 1833, we were to say good-bye to low life for ever. And with it how much vigour went ! No more bulldogs, no more terriers, except of the most exceptional breed and in the most picturesque positions ; no more " Fighting Dogs getting Wind," no more dogs of poor men even, except Highland shepherds. Though it was time that the high art should die after its failure in "Chevy Chase" we cannot help wishing that high life had not so completely taken its place. At the same time we must own that we got something better—not only high life but high thoughts, not only refinement of manners but of sentiment, not only "society" but "poetry." Yet we miss the vigour—which now disappeared, only to flash out again once more, but magnificently, near the last, in " The Swannery invaded by Eagles."

Now his soul was possessed by the majesty and beauty of Scotch scenery to a far greater extent than would be traceable from his pictures alone. That this was so is evident from the number of fine drawings of pure landscape, drawn at this time (1829—30), of which we are able to give some notion in our woodcuts. This chapter is illustrated with no less than six of these (Figs. 44—48 and PLATE XIV.), all belonging to these two years. They are, with one exception, in oil. They are all grand and

FIG. 44.—A RIVER IN SCOTLAND (1829).

solitary, all truly illustrations of " Caledonia stern and wild, meet nurse for the poetic child." In losing the colour of landscape we lose so much that it is dangerous to comment upon what remains, and we shall, therefore, leave our readers to gather what thoughts they may from this series, only pointing out how varied are the atmospheric effects, and how fine the composition of them all, both with regard to form and chiaroscuro. If he neglected landscape in his boyhood it now had a full

revenge; and if he obtained the assistance of Callcott to paint the landscape of a
picture—as he did in 1833 ("Harvest in the Highlands")—it was not for the same
reason that he sought that office from Nasmyth in 1822 ("The Bull and the Frog"),
namely, that he had not sufficient experience to do it so well himself.   We doubt,
however, if it be ever worth while for artists to work in this sort of partnership: the
landscape is nearly sure to be out of feeling with the figures.

Henceforth the beauty of most of Landseer's pictures was as dependent upon the
landscape as the animals, and his thoughts were as much occupied with one as the other,
which gave a larger scope to his powers of composition and the exercise of the more

FIG. 45.—SCOTTISH LAKE-SCENE (1829—30).

poetical part of his imagination.   In his landscapes as in his animals there was always
observable the same oneness of conception, the same dignity of character, and the same
harmony of feeling, and in his pictures, where both were introduced, they were fused
together into one idea.   It was no question of putting in a background to an animal or
figures into a landscape—such hybrid productions were impossible to him; the whole
picture was one, and would have been almost as much spoilt by the omission of a branch
as of the leg of a dog.   The grand forming power of his mind was never better illustrated
than in the magnificent sketch of a composition in PLATE XIII. (1829—30), which is
called "Rest," where a deerstalking party have thrown a dead stag across the fork of
a withered tree and are resting or waiting with their dogs.   We wonder that Landseer

THE MOUNTAIN STREAM (1829—30).

PLATE XIV.

never made use of this splendid suggestion, which appears to us to be almost unique in design.

With two more sketches of Highland interiors (PLATE XV.), 1831, and one of a "Deerstalker" (Fig. 49), the series of our artist's Scotch studies comes for the present to the end. In 1831 he was elected to the full honours of an Academician, and to this year belong the sketches of the head of Sir Walter Scott (Fig. 33). In the Academy of that year he exhibited "Interior of a Highlander's Home," and at the British Institution "The Highland Cradle," a picture for which the drawings on PLATE XV. were probably

FIG. 46.—A SCOTTISH LANDSCAPE (1829—30).

studies. In this year he also exhibited (at the Royal Academy) the "Poacher's Bothy" and "Poachers Deerstalking," which we mention here, as it has been suggested that the drawing (Fig. 49) was a portrait of a celebrated poacher, either Charles Mackintosh or Malcolm Clarke, portraits of both which notorieties were included in the latter picture, which is better known under the names of "Getting a Shot" and "Waiting for the Deer to rise," which have been given to the engravings from it. There is at all events so much similarity in the thought and arrangement of the two compositions as to make it interesting to compare the sketch with the picture, though if the date given to the former be correct it could not possibly be a study for the latter.

P

revenge; and if he obtained the assistance of Callcott to paint the landscape of a picture—as he did in 1833 ("Harvest in the Highlands")—it was not for the same reason that he sought that office from Nasmyth in 1822 ("The Bull and the Frog"), namely, that he had not sufficient experience to do it so well himself. We doubt, however, if it be ever worth while for artists to work in this sort of partnership: the landscape is nearly sure to be out of feeling with the figures.

Henceforth the beauty of most of Landseer's pictures was as dependent upon the landscape as the animals, and his thoughts were as much occupied with one as the other, which gave a larger scope to his powers of composition and the exercise of the more

FIG. 45.—SCOTTISH LAKE-SCENE (1829—30).

poetical part of his imagination. In his landscapes as in his animals there was always observable the same oneness of conception, the same dignity of character, and the same harmony of feeling, and in his pictures, where both were introduced, they were fused together into one idea. It was no question of putting in a background to an animal or figures into a landscape—such hybrid productions were impossible to him: the whole picture was one, and would have been almost as much spoilt by the omission of a branch as of the leg of a dog. The grand forming power of his mind was never better illustrated than in the magnificent sketch of a composition in PLATE XIII. (1829—30), which is called "Rest," where a deerstalking party have thrown a dead stag across the fork of a withered tree and are resting or waiting with their dogs. We wonder that Landseer

THE HIGHLAND MOTHER (1831).

THE HIGHLAND CRADLE (1831).

PLATE XV.

never made use of this splendid suggestion, which appears to us to be almost unique in design.

With two more sketches of Highland interiors (PLATE XV.), 1831, and one of a "Deerstalker" (Fig. 49), the series of our artist's Scotch studies comes for the present to the end. In 1831 he was elected to the full honours of an Academician, and to this year belong the sketches of the head of Sir Walter Scott (Fig. 33). In the Academy of that year he exhibited "Interior of a Highlander's Home," and at the British Institution " The Highland Cradle," a picture for which the drawings on PLATE XV. were probably

FIG. 46.—A SCOTTISH LANDSCAPE (1829—30).

studies. In this year he also exhibited (at the Royal Academy) the "Poacher's Bothy" and "Poachers Deerstalking," which we mention here, as it has been suggested that the drawing (Fig. 49) was a portrait of a celebrated poacher, either Charles Mackintosh or Malcolm Clarke, portraits of both which notorieties were included in the latter picture, which is better known under the names of "Getting a Shot" and "Waiting for the Deer to rise," which have been given to the engravings from it. There is at all events so much similarity in the thought and arrangement of the two compositions as to make it interesting to compare the sketch with the picture, though if the date given to the former be correct it could not possibly be a study for the latter.

P

Our next woodcut, despite the dead deer, belongs to an entirely different class of Landseer's work, and is connected with an important fact in his life and career, to which we have only at present casually alluded, viz., that, more than any artist of his time, his works were valued and his society sought by the aristocracy.   As a boy he had always made friends, and must have been distinguished by attractiveness, not only

FIG. 47.—LAKE SCENE IN SCOTLAND (1829—30).

artistic but personal, and when in 1824 he became the guest of Sir Walter Scott at Abbotsford he was already distinguished by his social no less than his artistic popularity.   He had before this become acquainted with the Duke and Duchess of Bedford, and in the same year he executed the first* of a series of portraits of their

---

* In the previous year (1823) he had painted a portrait of Georgiana, Duchess of Bedford, which was engraved for " The Keepsake."

family which was to extend to 1844. His first picture was called "The Bedford Family," and contained the portraits of two boys and two girls, with a white horse, in a Highland landscape. He next painted the well-known "Lord Cosmo Russell on his Pony Fingal," then "Lady Louisa Russell feeding a Donkey," and no less than three pictures of Lord Alexander, with different pet dogs. The next year (1826) he painted "Lady Louisa Russell, with Lady Rachael," and the "Duchess of Bedford on a Pony." Many of these and many other of Landseer's works were etched by

FIG. 48.—LAKE SCENE (1829—30).

Georgiana, Duchess of Bedford. In the same year, not forgetful of his old friends, he drew a portrait of the coachman of his old friend Mr. Simpson. In 1827 he painted the "Hon. James Murray (second son of Lord Glenlyon), with a Gamekeeper and Favourite Fawn," and in 1828 his first portrait of a Cavendish, in "The Chieftain's Friends," in which was a likeness of Lord Richard Cavendish, with a favourite greyhound and hawks. The same year at the Royal Academy was exhibited a "Scene in the Highlands," with portraits of the Duchess of Bedford, the Duke of Gordon, and Lord Alexander Russell. The next year (1829) he painted his own likeness as "The

Falconer," which was engraved for *The Amulet*, and again that of Lord Alexander Russell, this time the well-known picture of the young lord on his pony Emerald, which he is jumping over a fallen tree; also the "Death of a Stag in Glen Tilt," containing portraits of John, fourth Duke of Athole, of the Hon. George Murray, John Crerar, Macintyre, and Charles Crerar. In 1831 he again painted Lady Rachael and Lady Louisa Russell, the former in the well-known picture of "Red Riding Hood" the latter in "Cottage Industry." The same year he painted the Duke of Aberdeen. The next

FIG. 49.—THE DEER-STALKER (1833).

year (1832) Lady Rachael Russell was painted three times: twice with her pet fawn Harty and once as the "Actress at the Duke's;" and the Duke of Devonshire twice: with Lady Constance Grosvenor, and with Lord and Lady Cavendish and dead deer. From a sketch for this picture our engraving (Fig. 50) is taken.

In the same year died Sir Walter Scott, of whom Landseer made a posthumous sketch, to be amplified next year (1833) in his picture of the poet seated in Rymer's Glen, with his three dogs Maida, Ginger, and Spice, the two latter being descendants of Pepper and Mustard, the one yellow and the other black.   His portraits of Sir A. W. Callcott, R.A., a study for the monk in " Bolton Abbey in the Olden Time," and the " Carington Children," also belong to 1833.   To complete our list of his portraits down to the end of the period over which this chapter extends must be added " Lady Georgiana Russell" and the " Marchioness of Abercorn and Child," both engraved for the " Book of Beauty," and the " Hon. E. S. Russell and Brother," all of the year 1834.

All this high society could not but have an enduring effect upon his art, for his

FIG. 50.—THE DUKE OF DEVONSHIRE AND LORD AND LADY CAVENDISH (1832).

distinguished sitters were not only his "patrons," but (especially the Bedford family) his companions and friends ; and it had this effect : it produced a refinement and elegance in his way of looking at things and composing his pictures. In many respects this was a gain, and in others a loss, as we have previously hinted, and we cannot reckon among the gains such pictures as the "Bolton Abbey in the Olden Time," "The Return from Hawking," and others of the same class, in which the spirit of the "olden time" is entirely subservient to prettiness and grace. We can fancy the shade of Sir

Q

Walter Scott smiling sadly at the scenes which he would have painted with so much more of vigour and truth.

The woodcut (Fig. 50) is therefore remarkable in our series as the first in which we find portraits of members of that distinguished society which was to have so much influence over Landseer's genius, and it is also to be noted as the first drawing we present in which he has used architecture as an important part of the composition. As probably one of the first suggestions of his celebrated picture of " Bolton Abbey " (a picture which perhaps, notwithstanding our remarks, has been more popular than

FIG. 51.—THE EMPEROR FOUNTAIN AT CHATSWORTH (1832—34).

any other of his works) it has another claim to our interest. Bolton Abbey is one of the seats of the Duke of Devonshire, and it was probably while staying there that Landseer first conceived the idea of the picture. As a companion to it we give a scene from another of the residences of the Duke, showing the celebrated " Emperor " fountain (Fig. 51) at Chatsworth.

The year 1834 was one of great importance, not only for the production of the celebrated "Bolton Abbey" and the "Courtyard," but also for three other well-known pictures, one of which is only equalled by "The Old Shepherd's Chief Mourner"

The Falcon (1834).

Plate XVI.

in the truth of its pathos and the greatness of its conception. This picture is "Suspense," where a splendid bloodhound is watching with anxiety at the closed door which shuts him out from his wounded master. The master is not visible, but the story is perfectly told. On the table lie his gauntlets, on the floor the blood-stained feather of his crest, while an ominous track of blood-spots leads up to the door. Of a very different kind was his "Naughty Boy," now in the Sheepshanks collection at South Kensington, and too well known to need description. We only mention it here as showing how various and vigorous was his work of this year. The other was a "Collie Dog

FIG. 52.—A COURTYARD (1834).

rescuing a Sheep from Snow," of which we in our chapter on dogs give a cut from the sketch. We do not agree with those who think that the powers of Landseer culminated in this year, for we believe his later pictures of deer touched a higher level of thought than even "Suspense;" but it was a year in which he showed a greater variety of power in full maturity than in any previous year, for in addition to the pictures mentioned he painted the "Highland Breakfast," now also in the Sheepshanks collection. We regret that we have no other specimens of his work to give in illustration of this year than "A Courtyard" (Fig. 52) and "The Falcon" (PLATE XVI.), a sketch from a well-known group in the "Bolton Abbey" which has frequently been engraved as a separate subject.

The period of ten years which our chapter covers may, however, with the exception already mentioned, be considered as that in which his genius ripened to its full maturity, and the progress which he made in that time, in extending the range of his art, is quite as astonishing as the previous development of his technical skill. But a great change had come over him. His studies of lions and of cattle bore no fruit in these years, except in their contribution to his artistic education. His studies of horses and donkeys produced little or nothing. His ambition after "high" art had died a natural death. Of all his early animal friendships only the dog remained in full force, and even he was regarded less for his own sake than as the friend of man and as an object of beauty or humour. But on the other side, how much he had gained! He had added the deer to his list of animals; he had studied nature in its noblest and wildest scenes; he had learnt to attach a human interest to all he saw or painted; he had greatly developed the power and range of his humour, and had become a man and a poet as well as an artist and a sportsman.

FIG. 53.—STUDIES IN BELGIUM (1840).

CHAPTER IV.

1834—44.

E have hitherto been able to illustrate the art-life of Landseer by studies which record his progress step by step. In the first chapter we were able not only to record but to show it pretty plainly. Our engravings, though necessarily missing a good deal of the peculiar delicacy of his work, yet demonstrated an advance in technical skill and in conquest of subject almost one by one. We then arrived at a point in which he had attained such mastery that improvement was only to be looked for in variety and composition, and after that, when the purpose for which his sketches were taken changed—viz., when they became less of studies for learning than studies for pictures—we were able, in the second and third chapters, to present sketches which were interesting as being connected in some way with the pictures with which he was achieving his fame. Now, however, we can

no longer do one or the other.   As to technical skill, it has long been impossible, and
as to his pictures, our sketches, though numerous enough, do not present a sufficiently
unbroken sequence chronologically to do more than sustain a comment on his career.
On the other hand we are able to give such a number of sketches of 1840 as can seldom
be gathered together from one year's harvest of one artist.   They are also sketches of
peculiar interest, as those made during his only absence (at least of any length) from his
native country, and when his mind was lying comparatively idle—not endeavouring to
please anybody but himself, or brooding over grand compositions, but having plenty of
time to draw what pleased him.   We therefore cannot regret that our series, as a record
of his career, is here in a measure broken.   The pictures which made the steps in it are
too well known to make studies of them necessary to give the reader a notion of them,

FIG. 54.—THE FERRY (1836).

which is all they could do ; and instead of this the numerous sketches of the year 1840
—made in ill-health, away from home—enable us as it were to live with him as he was,
if not as a man, at least as an artist.   As a man, no ; for his character is only to be
seen clearly by taking a large view of his whole work, and of his inner life that work
shows us little or nothing except when aided by other knowledge, and even then not
much ; but as an artist, yes ; for these sketches show this part of his nature even better
than his finished pictures ; for in the latter he was not an artist merely, but a man of the
world, a poet, and a humorist, and in looking at them our interest is engaged by considerations which divert it from their purely artistic merit.   In these sketches, however,
Landseer is nothing but an artist, and to those that can feel the direct pleasure which
comes from seeing work in which every touch is a masterly exercise of high power
highly trained, in which the hand expressed perfectly and unfalteringly the image in the

STUDY OF FIR-TREES (1840).

PLATE XVII.

mind, with a consensus rarely felt except between voice and music, they will not need any humour or sentiment to heighten their satisfaction.

But before we come to these sketches, of which Fig. 53 is a foretaste, there are some achievements of the time between the date with which our last chapter closes (1834) and the year in which they were executed (1840), which require some notice here, as showing new developments of the artist's power. The first of these is "The Highland Drover's Departure," which was exhibited at the Royal Academy in 1835, and which

FIG. 55.—A FALCONER (1837).

has since become the property of the nation through the gift of Mr. Sheepshanks. This picture belongs to the same class of his work as his "Harvest in the Highlands," but it is distinguished from that picture by the fact that it is wholly painted by Landseer—whereas Callcott contributed the landscape to the other work—and also by the superior interest of the human figures. It is the first picture of importance by Landseer in which this interest (if we except the "Whiskey Still," in which the interest is mainly human) is quite equal, if not superior, to that of the animals, and this, although the studies of brute life are unusually varied and amusing.   In the sympathy

FIG. 56.—A SKETCH AT WINDSOR CASTLE (1838).

exhibited with the ordinary life of the Scottish peasantry it resembles Wilkie, and is the prototype of the series of pictures of scenes in Scotland with which Mr. Thomas Faed has so often delighted us. In it he first fairly showed the variety of his powers in one composition: feeling for nature in the beautiful landscape; truth and character

FIG. 57.—THE QUEEN ON HORSEBACK (1838.)

of animals in the sheep, ponies, &c.; humour in the puppy and the hen; pathos in the breaking up of the family party; sentiment—and manly sentiment too—in the lovers; and all were painted admirably and grouped with charming effect. In this year

(1835) he also produced his most wonderful picture of the "Sleeping Blood-hound"
—a posthumous portrait of Mr. Jacob Bell's dog Countess.   This work stands almost
alone, even among Landseer's, for grandeur and simplicity of design.   It is only a
dog, and the dog is sleeping—that is, expressionless : a picture which has no interest
except for its form ; but that is fine enough to place it amongst Landseer's greatest
achievements, in painting or sculpture—to which severer form of art it rather belongs,
for it is more conspicuous for the massiveness of its modelling and the harmony of its
lines than for its beauty of colour.

The next year (1836), to which our little cut of " The Ferry " (Fig. 54) belongs,
was not remarkable for any great picture, or any specially interesting to us, though

FIG. 58.—A HIGHLAND BOTHIE (1840).

the picture of "Comical Dogs," exhibited in the British Institution, was the first
picture in which he indulged in pure travesty ; the humour, such as it is, being not
inherent in the animals themselves, but in the way they are dressed up and in the
expressions forced upon their faces.   It is not the dogs which are comical, but the
artist.

In 1837 appeared, at the Royal Academy, the " Return from Hawking," "The
Hawk," and " The Peregrine Falcon," only interesting to us in connection with our
cut of " A Falconer," a drawing of the same year (Fig. 55) ; but the same exhibition
contained " The Old Shepherd's Chief Mourner,"* one of the most nobly pathetic

* " Here the exquisite execution of the glossy and crisp hair of the dog, the bright, sharp touching of the
green bough beside it, the clear painting of the wood of the coffin and the felds of the blanket, are language

REFRESHMENT: BELGIUM (1840).

THE NOONDAY MEAL: GENEVA (1840).

PLATE XVIII.

pictures ever painted. This picture has been beautifully, though not very accurately, described by Mr. Ruskin in "Modern Painters," vol. i., p. 8. We say "not very accurately," because the dog's breast is against the blanket, and not against the wood ; the blanket is not on the trestle, but the coffin ; the spectacles do not mark the place where the Bible was last closed ; and the dog must have moved "since the last blow was struck on the coffin lid," or he could not, as Mr. Ruskin says, "have dragged the blanket off." But the eloquence and real truth of the passage are too great for us to venture upon another, even if it were needed. It will be sufficient for our purpose to

FIG. 59.—WOODCUTTERS (1840).

say that it is Landseer's most perfect poem of simple pathos. The depth of the feeling expressed, which divides it from almost all his other pictures, will be seen by

---

—language clear and expressive in the highest degree. But the close pressure of the dog's breast against the wood ; the convulsive clinging of the paws, which has dragged the blanket off the trestle ; the total powerlessness of the head, laid close and motionless upon its folds ; the fixed and tearful fall of the eye in its utter hopelessness ; the rigidity of repose, which marks that there has been no motion nor change in the trance of agony since the last blow was struck upon the coffin-lid ; the quietness and gloom of the chamber ; the spectacles marking the place where the Bible was last closed, indicating how lonely has been the life, how unwatched the departure, of him who is now laid solitary in his sleep : these are all thoughts—thoughts by which the picture is separated at once from hundreds of equal merit, as far as the mere painting goes—by which it ranks as a work of high merit, and stamps its author, not as the neat imitator of the texture of a skin or the fold of a drapery, but as a Man of Mind."—*Modern Painters.*

comparing it with the picture of "Suspense," to which we alluded in our last chapter. Instead of the agony of anxiety, we have here the agony of hopelessness, of assured loss. Instead of impatient we have patient suffering. The story is told more fully, and the dog's master shares our sympathy. The picture is often called "The Shepherd's Chief Mourner;" but the omission of the word "old" takes away a great part of its meaning. What may be called the sequel to this picture was painted also in the same year, and named "The Shepherd's Grave," where a dog is mourning over his master's grave; and both of these pictures may be said to have their first

FIG. 60.—SHAKESPEARE'S CLIFF, DOVER (1840).

suggestion in the sketch of the dog howling on the shores of a lake, of which we made mention in the course of our remarks upon the year 1828. *

"A Distinguished Member of the Humane Society"—a further illustration of the services of the dog to man, and "There's Life in the Old Dog yet"—one of the few instances of the services of man to the dog—were his principal contributions to the Royal Academy next year, 1838; with "None but the Brave Deserve the Fair." And at the British Institution were exhibited the "Deer Family" and "Rabbit and

---

* Page 50.

Scene at Geneva (1840).

The Fountain: Geneva (1840).

Plate XIX.

Stoat."* The sketch for the last will be found on PLATE XXX. None of these pictures require special mention by us here, unless it be the "None but the Brave deserve the Fair," which perhaps contained the first idea for his later poems of "Night" and "Morning;" and at all events is interesting, and shows with what different spirits he looked upon "natural selection" in 1838 and 1853. But there was another picture exhibited at the Royal Academy, which marks a distinct step in his career, viz., "Dash, Hector, Nero, and Lorie," the pets of her Majesty the Queen. In 1835 he had painted the pony and the dogs of the present Duke of Cambridge, in

FIG. 61.—LAUNCHING THE BOAT, HASTINGS (1840).

a picture called "Prince George's Favourites;" and in 1839 he painted a portrait of the Queen, which was given by her Majesty to Prince Albert before her marriage. He had thus reached the Palace, and that not only as an artist: from this time to his death, we think that we are not wrong in stating that her Majesty not only favoured him with patronage but with personal regard.

In an article which appeared in a newspaper (*Daily News*) shortly after the death of the artist occurs a passage which it is interesting to quote here. "Many persons

---

* He exhibited twelve pictures this year—six at the Royal Academy and six at the British Institution; but we only mention in this and other years those pictures which are important to our design.

T

believe that Sir Edwin Landseer's attractive social qualities opened a communication between royalty and the intellectual accomplishment of the country. For some time after the Queen's accession the intellectual classes were markedly excluded from the Palace; and Landseer talked about it, like other people, and said that some change must by some means take place. The first familiar guest from the excluded classes was Edwin Landseer himself. In a little while St. John's Wood was amazed at the spectacle of the Queen waiting at Landseer's door while he changed his coat and mounted one of the groom's horses to ride with the Queen. The reason was that he

FIG. 62.—ON THE BEACH AT HASTINGS (1840).

was painting her Majesty on horseback, and this was a piece of professional study, devised impromptu by the royal sitter. Again, Prince Albert's hat and gloves* were seen on the floor of the artist's room—sent there without the Prince's knowledge, in order to be introduced into a portrait of his favourite dogs with which he was to be surprised on his birthday; and great was the bustle when a groom rode up, on a horse all in a lather, for the hat and gloves, as the Prince was going out, and must not miss

---

* Perhaps these were the hat and gloves so darkly alluded to by Mr. Stephens in p. 46 of his Memoirs.

his hat. In time came the autumn visits to Balmoral," when, we are informed in the same article, he "played billiards with the Prince," and "helped the Queen over stiles in her long walks." The effect of Royalty upon his art, as shown in Fig. 56 and Fig. 57, is not favourable; but these studies are interesting as containing what appears

FIG. 63.—A DONKEY DRIVER (1840).

to be the original conception of his portrait of her Majesty (one for which she did not sit), which was painted in the year of his death, 1873, or thirty-five years after.

In the next year (1839) appeared the first of his pictures of "Van Amburgh and his Animals," the only pictures in which he can be said to have thoroughly failed; but the subject was unworthy. In the same exhibition, however, he showed his real strength in "Dignity and Impudence"—one of his finest pictures both for humour and

dog-character—one which for force and truth of contrast and absence of caricature
reminds one of Hogarth at his best, and without his bitterness.

We now come to 1840, in which year he painted an otter (perhaps for the first time)
in a study for his large picture called "Otter and Salmon." It was exquisitely
engraved on wood by S. Williams for "Days and Nights of Salmon Fishing," by
William Scrope.* In this year "Laying down the Law" appeared: a fine and
amusing picture belonging to the class of the "Comical Dogs," in which the fun is in
the artist's treatment, and not in the nature of the dog—a distinction of much
importance in the intellectual rank of the picture, and one which, in our opinion,
divides it by a great gulf from "Dignity and Impudence."

In this year—to his misfortune, but for our present gain—he fell into ill-health, and

FIG. 64.—A DRAUGHT-HORSE: RAMSGATE (1840).

was recommended to travel. By what we daresay is nothing more than a coincidence,
our illustrations of this year indicate a restlessness, a frequent change of place, and
even suggestions of departure from England. From "A Highland Bothie" (Fig. 58),
"Llyn-y-Dinas" (tailpiece, Fig. 69), and the "Study of Fir-trees" (PLATE XVII.), he
appears to have visited Scotland and Wales; Fig. 60, "Shakespeare's Cliff," shows him at
Dover, Figs. 61—63 at Hastings, and Fig. 64 at Ramsgate; and there is reason to believe
that these sketches were made before he left England, as he did not do so till the autumn
of the year. However this may be, none of these sketches show any failure of power,
though the subjects of those at the seaside are not in his usual groove, as though done

* GRAVES, p. 25, No. 280.

in idle moments for pastime. Of these, the most peculiar is Fig. 58, with one of its figures with no head, and another which is "all head." The concealment of the head by the beam is intelligible, though quaint; but the gigantic wooden-looking character on the right, with a black periwig and no legs, is both odd and inexplicable—it is more like the old figurehead of a ship than a human being: while the group by the fire, the interlacing of the beams, the roosting fowls, and the light and shade, are full of interest and power. The next (Fig. 59) is almost equal to "Rest" (Plate XIII.) for its beauty of composition and fine drawing of the trunk. Even in our woodcut we can

FIG. 65.—At Church: Belgium (1840).

trace the accurate drawing of the cliffs and rocks of Fig. 60 ("Shakespeare's Cliff, Dover"); we can tell that these waveworn masses are soft and white—and the instinctive sense of harmony that has made beauty out of shapelessness and desolation. From Dover we come to Hastings, and there we find first a most vigorous sketch of men launching a boat. Note the different ways in which the six men are uniting to shove the boat off and keep her head straight. Two are pushing at the stern, two at the side are partly pushing and partly lifting, to ease her bottom off the shingle or sand; the other two, with their backs well set against her side, are keeping her head to sea. The attitudes of the men in the boat are equally expressive, and the whole

group, boat and all, is one living moving mass. But this sketch is not more
remarkable for variety of energetic action, unified by one desire, than the next sketch
(Fig. 62), "On the Beach at Hastings," is for variety of idle posture and the want of
a common will. One on the edge of the boat, one sitting with his back against it, two
lying on their right side, one on his left; two sitting apart, conversing, three absolutely
idle, unless they are looking out for some stray holiday maker who may want a sail.
These are the links of that strong human chain on the former page, separate and
useless for a while. The grouping of this drawing is no less happy than that of the
other. The next sketch, "A Donkey Driver" (Fig. 63), is very slight, but clever in
design, especially in the way the horns of the side-saddle are made to compose with the
donkey's ears. Our next sketch (Fig. 64) brings us to Ramsgate, and shows us
"A Draught-horse," which we think we must have seen, if not at Ramsgate, at some
other place by the seaside, toiling over the sand with a bathing machine behind it when
the tide was out.

In our next sketch we are fairly across the water, with new men and new animals.
But first let us turn back to "Studies in Belgium" (Fig. 53), where we shall see the
completeness of the change by two little humorous sketches. First, a contrast of
horses. That thin straightnecked animal in the corner is surely meant for an English
horse, something like the poor Draught-horse in Fig. 64; but face to face with him is
his continental brother, round everywhere, in neck, and barrel, and flank, as comfortable
and compact as the other is miserable and weedy. By their side is another contrast of
men and dogs, which reminds us of his early contrasts of the French and English pigs;
but here the palm of obesity must be given to the foreigners, both human and canine.
This contrast also suggests reminiscences of "High Life" and "Low Life." Above,
we see a horse, distinguished from his English relations not more by his breed than
his trappings, and by his side two men, of which the same may be said. Here, as in
the rest of his drawings abroad, may be seen how completely he caught the character
of the foreign types, human and animal.

In "At Church: Belgium" (Fig. 65), we have several studies of the poor at
their devotions, all touched in with a skilful and reverent hand—a group at the altar
rails, an old man telling his beads in the porch, and two seated figures of girls,
apparently muttering their aves and paternosters; but the most beautiful of all his
sketches of human character abroad is the "Market Scene" on PLATE XXI., taken,
we believe, at Aix-la-Chapelle, of which the full beauty, like that of all these sketches,
must be felt rather than described. For this reason we shall leave the reader to
wonder over the rest of them undisturbed by more than a few comments of ours. In
the sketches on PLATE XVIII. he will find two studies of animals eating, one of which,
"Refreshment, Belgium," was possibly the origin of a picture painted in 1846, and
called "Refreshment: a Scene in Belgium." On PLATE XIX. are two drawings of

RESTING (1840.)

THE DRAUGHT HORSE: GENEVA (1840).

PLATE XX.

FIG. 66.—A PUMP AT FRANKFORT (1840).

animals drinking, in both of which a great variety of life and other detail is introduced, and great care taken with their composition. It is strange that Landseer never reproduced them as pictures, as they are evidently much more than local studies, especially the " Scene at Geneva," in which the girl with the fish-basket reminds one of the girl in " Bolton Abbey in the Olden Time." Less elaborate, but quite as fine, as far as they go, are the studies on PLATE XX., while on PLATE XXI., besides the human group to which we have already alluded, there is a study of sheep quite marvellous in character and variety, even for Landseer. The feeling also of the

FIG. 67 —STUDIES AT GENEVA (1840).

solemnity, almost sacredness, of evening appears here for the first time, showing that a change, if not a shadow, had fallen on his spirit. This beautiful drawing is probably the origin of the picture without a name in the year 1845, which we all know so well under its engraved name of " The Shepherd's Prayer." The study of a " Pump at Frankfort " shows how much leisure he must have had to spend time in making record of a curiosity so completely out of his line. The animals in Figs. 67 and 68 require no words to illustrate their faithful drawing.

At the close of the year Landseer returned to England better in health, and we

SHEPHERDS OF STRASBURG (1840).

A MARKET SCENE (1840).

PLATE XXI.

are inclined to think that the "Woodcutters" (Fig. 59) may have been executed after his visit to the Continent, as the scene is a wintry one and full of strength and enjoyment of exercise—qualities which are not observable in his foreign sketches, despite their rare beauty, or even in the previous sketches of the year. In the next year he exhibited no picture, but in 1842 he appeared again in full vigour with his "Otter and Salmon," and "The Sanctuary" at the Royal Academy, and "Be it ever so humble, there's no place like home," at the British Institution. He also drew in this year his first design for "The Challenge," so that this year may be taken as

FIG. 68.—SWISS MULES (1840).

the commencement of his pictures of deer, remarkable for their sad, spiritual suggestiveness. The deerstalker had given place to the poet, and the gladness of action to the solemnity of reflection.

In 1843 he painted his "Defeat of Comus" for the Queen's summer-house in Buckingham Palace Gardens, of which a sketch was left to the nation by Jacob Bell; a picture of terrible force, and the first in which he showed his power in the domain of pure fancy. The next year appeared the "Challenge" and the "Otter Hunt," a sketch for which fine but painful picture is engraved on PLATE XXII.

x

In the ten years through which this chapter extends he may be said to have executed his finest work of pure pathos, his finest statuesque study of a dog, his best picture of Highland character, and a most beautiful series of sketches abroad. He had also commenced his pictures of spiritual poetry and pure fancy; but he had passed through a severe illness, and his art had become more thoughtful if not more sad.

FIG. 69.—LLYN-Y-DINAS (1842).

The Otter Hunt (1844.)

PLATE XXII.

FIG. 70.—LOCH LAGGAN (1847).

CHAPTER V.

1842—73.

ANDSEER'S tour on the Continent appears to have had little effect upon his art. Until the year 1845, or five years after it, he does not appear to have used one of his studies for a picture. Neither the scenery, the inhabitants, nor the animals, seem to have affected his imagination to any appreciable extent. New scenes and associations had such a remarkable effect upon him when he went for the first time to Scotland in 1824 that we might have expected a different result, and any one who had looked over his portfolio on his return and seen the matchless series of studies, of which we have been able to give so many specimens, would have been justified in prophesying that they would give birth to as fine a series of pictures. But it was not so; either the depressing circumstances under which he travelled may have given him a distaste for the records of his travel, or it was too late for his mind to fertilise the new seed. However that may be, we find in his after-work no alteration in his subjects or his method of treatment, except such as belonged to changes, mental and physical, which he underwent : an increasing prevalence of sad and terrible thoughts in his finished compositions, accompanied by a broader and more philosophical spirit; and in his execution greater wonders of manual dexterity and less sound painting—the former no doubt due to his increasing attacks of depression, the latter partly to the failure of his eyesight.

But if the Continent did not greatly increase his range of art, we may be thankful

FIG. 71.—AN ENGLISH HOMESTEAD.

that it did not, as in the case of Wilkie and others, damage it. On the contrary, whatever effect it had was for good, and though we do not reckon as among his greatest works such pictures as "The Shepherd's Prayer," "Geneva," "Refreshment," "A Dialogue at Waterloo," and "The Maid and the Magpie," we should be sorry to miss them from the collection of our memory. The first of these appeared in the Royal Academy of 1845, without a title ; and in this year he painted for Mr. Vernon a picture, not large in size or important in subject, but which, as a piece of painting, he never excelled, viz., "The Cavalier's Pets," now in the National Gallery. "Refreshment" appeared the next year, in which also appeared his splendid "Stag at Bay," and the beautiful pair of "Peace" and "War," pictures which deserve

A Highland Mountain Stream.

Plate XXIII.

notice here as being the first in which he showed himself capable of moving us not only by the circumstances of individual life, but by scenes symbolizing the common lot of mankind—as a poet not only of men but of man, not only pathetic but reflective. It is only a true poet, and an original one, who could invest such well-worn subjects with such new interest. Is it not also a link between him and Hogarth, that we

FIG. 72.—THE FORESTER'S SON (1849).

do not so much look at as read some of his pictures?* How full of " matter " is the " Peace," with its beautiful background of fair green down speckled with sheep and its calm expanse of sunny sea, with its children playing at " cat's-cradle," and the lambs peeping into the rusty cannon's mouth! More wonderful even is the " War,"

* See Charles Lamb's " Essay on Hogarth."

Y

with its distance shut out with rolls of smoke, and the terrible ruin of man, beast, and home in the foreground.

The most notable picture of next year (1847) was "The Drive of Deer, Glen Orchay," of the sketch for which we give an engraving in PLATE XXXVIII., one of the finest and most original compositions of sport in the Highlands; but this year also produced his second (the Duke of Wellington's) picture of "Van Amburgh," which is worse than the first (the Queen's). To 1847 also belongs the sketch of

FIG. 73.—SITTING FOR A PORTRAIT.

"Loch Laggan" (Fig. 70), possibly made for a picture of "Her Majesty Sketching at Loch Laggan," which he executed this year, and which, like the sketch, is in the possession of the Queen. The year after (1848) was signalised by two pictures, equal in power and execution, but as opposite in sentiment as mirth and murder. From his first drawing of a dead stag to this terrible "Random Shot," where a little fawn is trying to suck its mother, that lies dead upon the snow, Landseer seemed to feel far more the sadness of destruction than the "glory of the chase," and at times, as in the game card at Woburn (1825), to which we have alluded in Chapter III., the cruelty

A Waterfall.

Plate XXIV.

of sport seems to have smitten him with its pain and compelled him to record it in all its naked horror. To such a nightmare of imagination we owe the almost unbearable torture of the "Otter Hunt" and the "Random Shot," and the still more heart-tearing picture of "Man proposes, God disposes" was surely born of a similar disease. Of all these pictures, however, the "Random Shot" is the wholesomest and the most pitiful. There is nothing sensational or savage about it: it is only too sad and too true. All these pictures, for the intensity of the horror of naked truth, can find an English parallel only in the works of Hogarth. Still more like that great master is the other and very different picture, "Alexander and Diogenes," an

FIG. 74.—THE DUCK POND.

extremely fine piece of burlesque, in which he has made his dogs truly actors, playing their parts in a human historical comedy. In the Diogenes we recognise one of the dogs in "Comical Dogs," little changed in expression, and in Alexander, with a subtle satire on the bumptious vulgarity of great people, the same type of animal as in "Low Life" and "Jack in Office." The solemn-looking flunkeys he has satirised with two bloodhounds of servile pomposity and magnificent physique, and the group of courtiers by dogs of various breeds, two of which—a dandy hound and a scandal-loving spaniel—are exchanging witty remarks to the disparagement of the philosopher of the tub.

The interest always taken by Landseer in peasant life is more frequently exhibited in his Scottish than his English sketches; but in "An English Homestead". (Fig. 71) we have a charming study of English farm-buildings and trees, with small but interesting groups of men and dogs. Landseer was always faithful to his early impressions. He lived and died in the residence in which he first "set up house" in St. John's Wood, improving it as his increasing means allowed, but never seeking to alter it. "Be it ever so humble," &c., may be said to have been his motto, notwithstanding his social distinction, and the depth of his family affections was never to be questioned. A beautiful instance of this is shown by his most loving and lovable picture of his old father executed in this year (1848), which alone would entitle him to a high rank amongst portrait painters. England always remained the land of his affections as Scotland was of his imagination: foreign countries were, as we have seen, powerless to lay hold of one or the other. Even the beauty of the scenery of Switzerland does not seem to have disturbed from their throne in his mind the glens of Scotland or the vales of England; for the one picture of "Geneva" we have many such scenes as those in our PLATES XXIII., XXIV., and XXV., the last of which is the most elaborate study of trees from his hand which we have seen.

In 1849 appeared the "Forester's Family"—a forester's wife followed by fawns, and preceded by her sturdy son, carrying a pair of antlers over his head in the manner shown in "The Forester's Son" (Fig. 72). In the picture the boy "is not seen as here represented, but rather sideways." * It is evidently a portrait, as is also Fig. 73, though this is a humorous one, reminding one again of Hogarth. If we put animals out of our consideration, Landseer was never more happy than when treating children.† Whether humble or wellborn, whether portraits or not, his feeling was always tender and true. The infant at the breast, as in "The Highland Breakfast," the child playing with his father's dirk in "The Drover's Departure," "H.R.H. Princess Alice in her Cradle," not to mention any others, are wonderful instances, not only of picturesque treatment, but of knowledge and observation, such as could scarcely be expected of a man who was not a father. They always have the true look and form of babies; not nambypamby, doll-like little creatures, but real sensible babies, with no grace but the true baby-grace—hard to appreciate and harder still to draw. In his studies of elder children, as in this "Forester's Son," and portraits like that of "Lord Alexander Russell" (PLATE XL.), he is equally successful in giving the character and spirit belonging to the age; and the exquisite grace and fancy of his portraits of young girls with their pets, such as the well-known "Beauty's Bath,"

---

* *Art Journal*, July, 1875.

† We use the words "happy" and "treating" in their artistic senses, but we have no doubt that the passage would be equally true if interpreted according to the ordinary use of the words.

STUDY OF OAK-TREES.

PLATE XXV.

"The Sutherland Family," and "Miss Blanche Egerton," with her cockatoo and bountiful hair, or in character, as "Little Red Riding Hood" (Lady Rachael Russell), and "Cottage Industry" (Lady Louisa Russell), the mention of which will immediately suggest others to the reader's mind, raise Sir E. Landseer to the highest rank as a painter of children. Without the colour or the subtlety of character which we see in Sir Joshua Reynolds or the superfineness of Sir Thomas Lawrence, they are quite equal

FIG. 75.—HOODED FALCON.

to the first in naturalness and to the second in real refinement, and are without the mannerism or affectation of either.

As to his portraits of men, the specimens we give of Sir Walter Scott and Paganini, and the portrait of his father to which we have alluded, are sufficient proof of his varied power. The sketch of "Paganini" (Plate XXVI.) again reminds us of Hogarth, not because it is, but because it is not, a caricature. The wild hair and action, the peculiar figure, the pocket-handkerchief, and eye-glass, are all, we are assured, "to

z

the life" without exaggeration. Nor were his portraits of ladies inferior in their way.
His contributions to the "Book of Beauty," and other portraits of noble ladies, show
a feeling for elegance which never degenerates into artificiality, and breathe an air
of distinction in which there is nothing of "fine-ladyism."

In 1850 appeared "A Dialogue at Waterloo"—a picture which had for some
years been expected by the public, who knew that it was one of those commissioned
by Mr. Vernon before his death. We do not know whether he visited the locality
between 1840 and 1850, but, at all events, the landscape was, we believe, studied
on the spot, and was the only contribution of importance which the Continent furnished
to Landseer's art.* The next year came "Midsummer Night's Dream" and "The
Monarch of the Glen," the former of which is the most beautiful "illustration" that
he ever painted. As a work of pure fancy, it ranks with his "Defeat of Comus,"
to which it is the natural companion in the history of his art-life. In these two
pictures he showed powers of fanciful imagination not exhibited before or after, and
that he could exercise it in opposite directions and enter into the spirit of others'
dreams. The two pictures are as different in sentiment as light from darkness : in
one a terrible orgy, of sensuality such as has never been painted in such repulsive
force before, if we except the prints of Hogarth ; in the other the liveliest frolic, the
most light-hearted mirth that the youngest fancy could conceive. The figure of
Titania is not fairylike enough, but the sprites and elves are as full of tricksy mirth
almost as Cruikshank's. These two pictures are, as we have said, natural companions. They show the two extremes of terror and joy between which his fancy
ranged. They are the "Peace" and "War" of his imagination—the "Night" and
"Morning" of his soul.

It is pleasant to think that, shaded as the concluding years of his life were by
clouds which at times almost concealed his reason, the bright side of his mind—his
humour and spirit—never altogether deserted him. When near his end, and occupying
himself at times with drawing reminiscences of his former pictures, it was not gloomy
or terrible thoughts that his pencil traced, but his "French Hog" and "British
Boar," his "Old Dog (Trim) looks like a Picture," and other amusing or sunny
memories; and in his last years of work, "Man Proposes but God Disposes" (the
terribly suggestive picture (1864) where Arctic bears in their native ice-world
have disturbed the grave of one of the ill-fated Sir John Franklin's ill-fated companions) has for its complement the playful picture of a bullfinch and squirrels, with
its jocose title, "Piper and a Pair of Nutcrackers." In 1869, the two currents of his
mind were still undivided, as was seen in the "Ptarmigan Hill" and "The Swannery
invaded by Eagles," a picture of magnificent power, in which his youthful fire and

* It was also used in "The Shepherd's Prayer."

NICOLO PAGANINI (1840).

PLATE XXVI.

ambition seem to flare out unexpectedly at the last. In 1872 came two pictures prophetic of death, both in the evident decay in the master's physical power and the religious solemnity of their subjects—"The Font" and "The Lion and the Lamb:" One also was prophetic in another sense, viz., a translation into form of the dream of the Hebrew seer of a time when "the lion shall lie down with the lamb." This picture reminds us of Blake, in the naked simplicity and the unsophisticated grandeur of its design, and the original drawing was even more like in spirit to the author of the "Tiger," for in it the lamb is lying on one of the paws of the lion, as a child lies on its nurse's arm. This was the last effort of his imagination. In the following year, on the 1st of October, he died, aged seventy-one.

So ended the history both of his life and his art, any notice of which would scarcely be complete without mention of his large and elaborate composition of 1860,

FIG. 76.—MACAWS.

called "Flood in the Highlands," which Mr. Stephens rates as "probably the strongest of all his pictures."[*] It is not the purpose of this book to deal with his life, nor have we materials to do so if we would. In our rapid and, we fear, very incomplete survey of his art, we have endeavoured to show the gradual development of it (1) in skill, (2) range of subject, (3) in thought, and we have purposely refrained from a lengthy disquisition upon any point, in order not to detain the reader upon the road; but now we have reached the end of our journey there are a few points which deserve greater attention than we were able to pay to them at the time, and

----

[*] Page 131.

a few that we have purposely passed without any notice at all.   To the most important
of the former, viz., his treatment of dogs and deer—we propose to devote separate
chapters, in which, if we fail to add anything new, we shall be able, at least, to sum
up and emphasize the remarks scattered through the foregoing pages.   To these we
shall add a short chapter upon his horses, more by way of contrast than on account
of their importance.   For the rest of this chapter we have selected a few of his
sketches, to illustrate a few facts of minor importance, but of much interest with
regard to his life.

The first of these is his treatment of birds, animals which, with the solitary exception of the study of vultures (Fig. 29), he drew with unvarying skill.   One of his
earliest drawings was a very neat one of a parrot in pencil, and one of his last
pictures was entirely devoted to birds—the "Swannery attacked by Eagles."   In
Figs. 74, 75, and 76 we have studies of ducks, a falcon, and macaws, all undated.
We cannot remember any picture in which Landseer introduced tame ducks, but this
is probably due to ignorance or defective memory; but wild ducks are introduced
with great effect into some of his pictures, and in one, "The Widow" (1825), they
form the subject.   This honour was, if we mistake not, shared only by eagles and
swans, if we except his studies of game.   Besides the picture so often mentioned, in
which these two birds are associated in one grand composition, he painted a small
picture called "The Eagle's Nest" (1833), presented to the nation by Mr. Sheepshanks, in which the bird, sitting on a ledge of bare rock, and surrounded by the
desolation of the mountain-tops, is very similar to that of "An Eagle" (Fig. 84).
Other birds he only introduced as objects of subsidiary interest into his compositions,
but they were always painted with wonderful dexterity; indeed, in no animals did
he show greater skill in representing the texture and substance than in his birds.
His feathers were feathers, not only in colour and lightness and drawing, but in
consistency; his beaks and talons were exact in their degree of horniness as in their
outline.   His use of them in his compositions was varied and always effective.   No
one who knows the pictures will forget the hen and chickens in the "Drover's
Departure" and "The Highland Shepherd's Home," the swan in "Bolton Abbey,"
the wild-fowl in "The Sanctuary," or the gulls in "Time of Peace."   His pictures
of hawking are well-known, and his macaws, cockatoos, and other pet birds, suggest
at once the names of the several children and ladies into whose portraits they were
so charmingly introduced.

The only quarrel we have against the pets, ornithological or otherwise, is the
time that was spent in painting them which might have been devoted to works of
more general, enduring, and noble interest.   His illustrations to the "Waverley
Novels," and his fine pictures from "Comus" and the "Midsummer Night's Dream,"
suggest that he left comparatively unworked one of the richest veins of his mental

STUDY OF RAMS' HEADS (1845).

STUDY OF RAMS' HEADS (1845).

PLATE XXVII.

wealth. This view is confirmed by the sketch in illustration of "The Lady of the Lake" (Fig. 37), and our next two woodcuts, "Friar Tuck" and "Don Quixote and the Lions" (Fig. 78), both of which are full of vigour and character, especially the . latter, which contains the elements of a picture singularly suited to the display of his varied power. That he fully appreciated the form and character of Sancho Panza is shown by his picture of that worthy, bequeathed to the nation by Mr. Sheepshanks, and he had too much fine feeling for literature and for all that was noble and chivalrous not to make us sure that his Don would have done justice both to the author and the knight; but whether or not our expectations as to the master

FIG. 77.—FRIAR TUCK (1834).

would have been confirmed, we have no hesitation in saying that his Rosinante was a loss to the world. In the sheet of these hasty sketches will be seen what was to have been the "car with the flags," which contained the "two fierce lions, which the general of Oran is sending to Court, as a present to his Majesty. Larger never came from Africa into Spain. . . . They are hungry, not having eaten to-day. . . . At which Don Quixote, smiling a little, said, 'To me your lion whelps! Your lion whelps to me! By the living God, those who sent them hither shall see whether I am a man to be scared by lions!'" Below is seen a sketch of the Don, who determined to fight the lions on foot, lest Rosinante should be terrified at the

A A

sight of them. " Upon this he leaped from his horse, flung aside his lance, braced
on his shield, and drew his sword ; and marching slowly, with marvellous intrepidity
and an undaunted heart, he planted himself before the car, devoutly commending
himself first to God and then to his mistress, Dulcinea." The three mounted figures
are evidently intended for Don Diego de Miranda on his mottled-grey mare, Sancho
on his donkey, and the carter on a mule, endeavouring to get well out of the way
before the cage is opened. The ultimate form which the composition was intended
to take is hardly indicated in the scattered sketches, two of which do not seem to

FIG. 78.—DON QUIXOTE AND THE LIONS.

belong to the same subject as the rest. We should have liked to see even such a
rough sketch of it as that for a composition, never to be completed, of " Friar Tuck."
In this, with a few rough pencil lines, he has sketched out a picture complete in its
grouping and even in many of its details. How much can be indicated by a few
dexterous touches was never better shown than in the figure on the left, seated upon
a dead stag, and the two dogs on the right, though the masterly sketch for the
" Otter Hunt" (PLATE XXII.) displays the same extraordinary power. They both,
and many others in our collection, exhibit that gift of conception that made Land-

BISON.

A BISON.

PLATE XXVIII.

seer's pictures spring in living unity from his brain like Minerva from the head
of Jupiter.   Except in cases in which the subject was not spontaneous, as the
"Dialogue at Waterloo," or when a design had to be altered to suit a special
purpose, as in his drawing of "The Beggar," there are no signs of labour in the
composition, no putting together of parts: they were all births, rather than construc-
tions.   This power of conception was so strong and varied, that in looking back

FIG. 79.—CONFESSION.

over his very numerous works it is hard to find one which suggests another in
its arrangement.   One instance of this in his early years we have mentioned,* and
another may be found in the two compositions on PLATE XXX. (the " Hare and
Foxes " and "The Feast interrupted ") one of which belongs to 1824 and the other
to 1838, and no doubt others may be found; but as a rule, a new subject clothed
itself as naturally in a new form as a new idea in a new phrase.   This instinct of
composition is visible in his earliest works † and in his slightest sketches, such as

those just mentioned, or the "Donkey Driver" (Fig. 63), the slightest and hastiest
of all. In all his works, sketches or finished, we only know of one awkward composition—a study of deer, in 1820. It was the same in his details as in his
great compositions, many of which could be cut up into several pictures, perfect in
themselves, although they fit into their places without any assertion of individual
existence. As to his animals, they seem to group themselves—as indeed animals do, to

FIG. 80.—A GIPSY ENCAMPMENT.

the artist's eye; of instances of which this volume is full, from the first sketch on
page 1 to the study of three rams' heads on PLATE XXVII., which reminds one
of the group in "The Drover's Departure," and which for variety and beauty of line
and light and shade, is perhaps the most wonderful in this volume.

As examples of Landseer's mastery over his materials, and power of representing
every variety of texture and substance, the other study of rams' heads on the same

THE GREALOCH (1857).

SHETLAND PONY AND HOUND (1857).

PLATE XXIX.

plate is equally wonderful. Both of these are executed in black and white chalk upon rough paper, the grain of which has been taken advantage of by Landseer to heighten the effect and economize his labour. Even in our woodcut we perceive the fibre and strength of the horns, the softness of the mouths, and the cool fleshiness of the nostrils, while the drawing is simply perfect; and much the same may be said of the masterly studies of the bison in PLATE XXVIII., executed in the same way, and belonging to the same owner (the Duke of Westminster). In these studies his technical power may be said to have reached its superlative of mastery.

It is seldom that we come upon any of Landseer's studies without regret that

FIG. 81.—A RACE-COURSE.

they have not been worked up into pictures; but this is the case with Fig. 79. "Confession," in which he seems to have intended to supplement his picture of the St. Bernard mastiffs rescuing a traveller's body by another of a monk of that establishment rescuing a human soul. The successful execution of this idea did not lie within the range of Landseer's art, great as it was. Though, as we have seen, he could introduce into his pictures human figures admirably expressive of domestic humour and sentiment, and could paint portraits remarkable for their grace and character, his power of expression of deep emotion or spiritual feeling was as much

D B

confined to animals and scenery as Turner's to landscape. If we wish for grace we may turn to his female portraits; if for character, to his "Highland Whiskey Still" or his "David Gellatley;" if we wish for sentiment, to his "Drover's Departure" or his "Time of Peace;" and we shall find it in his human figures to a degree which will bear contrast with the animals; but if we want elevation of sentiment we must turn to "The Sanctuary;" if we want deep and sorrowful thought, to the "Night" and "Morning," or if we want faith, to "The Lion and the Lamb." The only exception

FIG. 82.—SKETCH OF A DOG (1871).

to this, and it is one that proves the rule, is the filial reverence and love that beam from every touch in his portrait of his father.

Landseer may be said to have had two countries—England and Scotland; the one of his affections, the other of his imagination. In the one he had been born and bred, had made his first studies and achieved his first reputation : he had wandered in her fields, and sketched her quiet cows and sheep, and made his first essays in landscape, of which Fig. 81 is probably one. In the other he had the first great impulse to his imagination : her mountains and glens inspired him with a love for beauty and wildness and solitude. The delight of being alone amongst magnificent scenery is constantly observable in his works, and in none more so than some of the landscapes in this

THE FEAST INTERRUPTED (1838).

HARE AND FOXES (1824).

PLATE XXX.

volume, or in his beautiful etching of "The Traveller's Rest." This led him to sympathize with the free wild life of poachers and gipsies, and gave birth to such compositions as "The Poacher's Bothy" and "A Gipsy's Encampment" (Fig. 80).* He may also be said to have had two tastes—love of sport and the love of animals. How these came into collision we have already shown, and how he never shrank from painting a scene because it was painful. We have tried to seek in the former part of this chapter for the reason of this latter peculiarity; but perhaps the real origin of it

FIG. 83.—SKETCH OF A STAG (1871).

was the inherent force of his artistic impulses, which prevented him from hesitating about the subjective effect which his work would produce. From the earliest time we find him studying and drawing in any place, and from any subjects which would afford food for his artistic appetite : at home, at the menagerie, in the fields, in the shambles, at the bull and bear baiting, he, with pencil in hand, drew insatiably, without regard to the sentiment, but only careful to represent it truthfully, whatever it was. So in later life he would draw such a study as that of "The Grealoch," where a man is

---

* The background of this picture is said to be similar to that in his picture of "The Bedford Family" (1824). See *Art Journal.*

beginning to skin a deer, or such a graceful group of pets as the "Shetland Pony and Hound" (PLATE XXIX.)—instinct with life, beauty, and happiness—with the same care and truth, both as to execution and feeling.

He also may be said to have had two brains, physical as well as intellectual : with regard to the latter pair, the artistic, and what, for want of a better antithesis, we may call the literary brain, we have already said much; but with regard to the apparent physical duality of his brain, its power of conducting two different operations at one and the same time, we have deferred observation to the present time as a matter

FIG. 84.—AN EAGLE (1852).

altogether beside our main object. It is, however, too remarkable a phenomenon, both from a scientific and an artistic point of view, to pass without notice, and we are able to produce ocular demonstration of the fact, viz., facsimiles of two sketches of different subjects produced simultaneously, the one with his left hand and the other with his right. That this was not a solitary instance of his exhibition of this remarkable power is evident from a story told by Mr. Stephens,* on the authority "of a Royal Academician of unquestioned sagacity, and remarkable for his accomplishments and acute powers of observation." The scene of Mr. Stephens's

---

* Pages 86, 87.

story is " the house of a gentleman not now unknown in the upper ranks of London society," and the feat performed is thus described : " A piece of paper was laid on the table, and Sir Edwin, a pencil in each hand, drew simultaneously, and without hesitation, with the one hand the profile of a stag's head and all its antlers complete, and with the other hand the perfect profile of a horse's head. Both drawings were full," Mr. Stephens continues, " of energy and spirit, and although, as the occasion compelled, they were not finished sketches, they were, together and individually, quite as good as even the master himself was accustomed to produce by one at a time, and with his right hand alone. The drawing by the left hand was not inferior to that by the right hand." We think our left-hand drawing (Fig. 82) is superior to the other (Fig. 83), but neither of them can be said to have the merit ascribed to the two mentioned by Mr. Stephens.

Landseer also had, as we all have, two spirits : one light and one dark, one gloomy and one gay, the one fearing and the other hoping. From first to last these alternated in his life and in his art, but the extreme of each was more intense than in ordinary mortals. Let the reader accept as the last types of these extremes (Figs. 84 and 85), the eagle tearing out the bowels of its prey, and the mother and child looking at the little chicks that are struggling towards a larger life.

FIG. 85.—LOOKING OUT.

FIG. 86.—CÆSAR.

CHAPTER VI.

DOGS.

T is not difficult to find many reasons why Landseer should have given us more pictures of dogs than of any other animals. One reason, sufficient of itself, is, that they are the best companions of man, and he, being eminently human, and caring about animals chiefly in their human relations, naturally made them his chief study. He may be said to have painted other animals as an artist, a poet, and a natural historian, and he, as such, painted also dogs ; but dogs alone he painted as a friend. We have in our first chapter expressed our opinion that the first animal he drew ought to have been a dog, and we have since discovered, what we should to have known before, viz., that the frame in the South Kensington Museum which holds nine early drawings of the boy Edwin, contains one (the earliest of them all) of a dog, executed at the age of five. It is apparently a fox-hound, and is altogether a marvellous production for a boy of his age—one of the artistic wonders of the world. After the death of his Brutus he despaired of finding another to take the place of that favourite, and said he would try to make up in quantity for the quality which he had lost, and ever afterwards was attended by a body-guard of several dogs ; as if to show the force of this habit, he has humorously drawn his own portrait with a dog on each side of him, apparently criticizing his work,—which would, we rather think, bear the criticism even of a dog. We speak diffidently, never having experienced the subjective impressions of a dog; but we cannot help believing that the manner in which Landseer drew the forms and expressed the character of the canine race would have been

FIG. 85.—A LETTER CARRIER (1842).

rewarded with the gratitude if not the full satisfaction of such a critic. He may occasionally have shown the artificial culture of the animal too much to please canine Conservatives; what he looked upon as cleverness they might despise as conceit; what he thought fineness of breed they might condemn as degeneration;

what he considered faithfulness they might rank as servility; what culture, as loss of caste; but on the whole, seeing that he was but a man, they must, we fancy, have allowed that he was a good artist, a fair judge of character, and meant kindly by them.

But to man he must now and, we think, ever, seem most profoundly learned in dog-nature, and the best dog artist that ever lived. Although "the essence of dog" may be, as Mr. Ruskin says somewhere, in Veronese's hounds, though Snyders excel in representing the savage onslaught of these animals in the chase, and though all Mulready's dogs are as good as Landseer's, yet no other artist has painted them in such variety, both of form and character, as he; none has represented the depth and

FIG. 88.—CORA (1821).

truth of their feelings so fully; none has devoted, as he did, a lifetime to their study, till he may be almost said to have "exhausted" the dog, as far as one man could. But the dog is as inexhaustible almost as man: his races are as many, his characters as diverse. He changes with every climate and with every need that man has for him in any shape. From the mastiff to the toy-terrier, from the greyhound to the turnspit, their differences of form, of habit, of instinct, of utility, are so various that any attempt to classify, let alone exhaust them, is a labour in comparison with which those of Hercules even seem puny.

One distinction of physical quality only shall we attempt to make, and this is, that

Dogs setting a Hare (1824).

The Angler's Guard (1824).

Plate XXXI.

all dogs may be classed under two heads: the hard dog and the soft dog.   To the former belong the deerhound, the greyhound, the collie, the bulldog, and the true terrier; to the latter, the mastiff, the bloodhound, the setter, and the spaniel.   In the one class the joints appear to be made of iron, and the sinews of whipcord; in the latter the joints appear loose, and the sinews but half-strung.   We are quite prepared to learn from someone better informed as to their anatomy that the difference which we have sought to draw is a mere optical illusion, due only to some external accident of looseness of skin or quantity of hair; but that will make no difference in the fact—

FIG. 89.—IN THE WARREN (1824).

illusion or not—that such a distinction exists, is justified by the general appearance of the animals, and is of such importance to the artist that we can easily conceive one who, being perfectly capable of representing to the life the jimp and wiry form of a black and tan terrier, would be puzzled to draw the loose and supple limbs of a setter.   That Landseer was an equal master of either, and that they are as much discriminated in his works as in those of nature, is no small praise to him as an artist.

We may, however, well take for granted that with regard to all physical pecu-liarities, whether of form or colour, hardness or softness, short hair or long hair, large hones or small bones, loose joints, or tight joints, breed or mongrelism, there was no difference, however slight, which he did not perceive, and was not able to transfer to canvas with a brush as deft as a magic wand.   We may also take for granted that there was scarcely any breed of dog, or dog of no breed, known in England during his lifetime, which did not at some time or other engage his pencil.   In these respects, at least, his treatment of the dog may be said to be almost exhaustive.   In this chapter alone we have Scotch terriers (Figs. 87 and 99, and PLATES XXXII. and XXXV.), Newfoundland (Fig. 86), Labrador (Fig. 88), English terriers (Figs. 89 and 90, and PLATE XXXII.), pointer (Fig. 91), deerhound (Figs. 92, 95, and 99, and

FIG. 90.—DOG (1825).

PLATE XXXV.), collies (Figs. 93, 94, and 96), nondescripts (Figs. 97 and 98), Dandie Dinmont (Fig. 99 and PLATE XXXV), setters, mastiff and greyhound (PLATE XXXI.), German badger-hound (PLATE XXXIII.), and beagle (PLATE XXXIV.).   All these dogs, and many more, did he draw, in every variety of posture and employment, and animated by every variety of canine sentiment.

   The only classification of interest to us is that of the different aspects in which the dog appealed to the interest of the artist; and first amongst these, let us place the dog as a masterpiece of natural organization.   From the first, whether a dog or other animal, Landseer's view was a complete one.   He took in the whole of it at once, and though

DOGS AT BAY (1828).

How now - a rat dead for a ducat!

ON THE WATCH (1830).

PLATE XXXII.

some parts may have been more truly drawn at first than others, there was seldom or ever any doubt as to its general appearance and character. His conception was always perfect, whatever his power of realizing it; and even in his earliest drawings any mistake is carried through the work with a kind of correlation of error, which preserved its unity, and made anything less than a facsimile a vitiation of the original, and this fact should always be borne in mind when observing any defects in our woodcuts. This gift of conception was the special mark of his genius, the basis of the unexampled success of his work, and the point in which it differs most essentially

FIG. 91.—AMONG THE HILLS.

from that of inferior artists. It is this that raises his "Sleeping Blood-hound" to the rank of sculpture, and gives artistic value to his merest portrait of a pet.

The next aspect in which dogs interested Landseer was as the possessors of a variety of natural habits and instincts. Their manners of walking, or bounding, or sleeping, or waking, every gesture of the paw or turn of the head or expression of the eye, the watchfulness of some, the laziness of others, their courage, their pugnacity, their pertinacity, their natural hatred of other animals, their fondness for each other, their marvellous gift of scent—all these and many more properties natural to the dog, formed a field of observation and study of which he was never tired. It is this which gives such variety and truth to his work that no two dogs from his hand ever seem alike, and which makes them interesting always as dogs, whatever the sentiment, human or otherwise, with which he may inspire them. His "Comical Dogs" would remain and be delightful as dogs without the mob-cap and the pipe, and his "Alexander" and any of his courtiers, cut out from the picture, would be nothing more than a dog, doggy from the expression of his eye to the curve of his tail. If he sometimes strained their faculty of human expression, it was only a

FIG. 92.— ON THE LOOK-OUT (1827).

strain, and not a wrench—exaggeration, if you like, of what was true, but never an addition of what was false. For illustrations of Landseer's sense of form and observation of natural habit, there is no need to go beyond the illustrations to this chapter. In "Cora" (Fig. 88) we have a dog hastily drawn, but magnificent in *pose*, and thoroughly characteristic in attitude. In "In the Warren" (Fig. 89) we have two studies of different views of the same dog, eager in pursuit of rats, and palpitating with excitement. Equally fine as examples of natural canine character are the "Dogs at Bay" and "On the Watch" on PLATE XXXII. But though Landseer never lost

HEAD OF DACHEL (1840).

PLATE XXXIII.

sight of the underlying natural canine character, he, comparatively early in his life, abandoned it as the one and sufficient motive of his composition. After 1824 we have no more "Fighting Dogs getting Wind," "Larders invaded," or "Impending Quarrels" (Fig. 23), but man asserts his right to be considered, even in relation to the dog.

The point of view from which the dog was of most interest to Landseer (at all events for the greater part of his life) was as the associate of man. The relations of the dog to man are so many and so different, that it is almost as difficult to classify them as their physical and moral varieties; but at all events, as far as Landseer

FIG. 93.—REAPERS RESTING: GLEN FISHIE (1827).

is concerned they may be divided into three heads: (1) companions, (2) servants, (3) pets. To Landseer the companionship of a dog seemed almost as necessary as a hat or a stick. A man was not complete without a dog, and a dog was scarcely complete without a man. He seldom—except in portraits, and not often in them— drew one without the other, or, at least, the suggestion of the other. Even his "Sleeping Bloodhound" has a helmet near—not a mere accessory, but a necessary part of the composition. It is not only the shepherd in the fields, the deerstalker at rest, that has his dog, but the fisherman on the beach, the whiskey distiller in the Highlands, and even the dustman; and all differ as their masters, so that you may

E E

almost know the man by his dog. The result of this companionship in raising the love of the dog to a degree hardly exceeded by human beings was the inspiration of some of Landseer's noblest thoughts and purest poetry—from his earliest to his latest work. The difference in feeling between "The Dustman's Dog" (Fig. 19), so patient of and subdued to his master's insignificance, and the "Dog howling on the Sea-coast," "The Old Shepherd's Chief Mourner," and "The Shepherd's Grave," is but a difference of degree, and "Suspense" is an example of the same devotion viewed in a romantic light.

As servants to man, if they did not suggest pictures of such deep sentiment,

FIG. 94.—A SHOWER IN THE HIGHLANDS (1828).

they suggested a greater number of them, and stimulate our admiration, if not our love, to the same degree. Their use in protecting our property, as shown in "Cora" and "Jack in Office;" their sagacity in rescuing from danger, as in the "Alpine Mastiffs reanimating a Distressed Traveller," or in "Saved," or in the "Distinguished Member of the Humane Society;" their invaluable assistance in our sports, whether in setting a hare, destroying rats, pulling down stags, or hunting an otter; their co-operation in gathering our sheep, and even digging them out of the snow; and the devotion of their eyesight to the poor blind man: these are some of the many instances in which Landseer showed his appreciation of the services of dogs.

Lastly as pets—dogs which give us pleasure for their beauty, or their amiability,

A BEAGLE.

PLATE XXXIV.

their cleverness, or their eccentricity, or as objects for the employment of surplus affection—dogs of which we should like portraits. Of these little need be said, for the qualities necessary to paint such pictures are included in those we have already mentioned as possessed by Landseer to a greater degree than any other animal painter before or since. Of them we give many examples in illustration of this chapter, all remarkable for their beauty and character, but none so wonderful as a masterly piece of sketching as the little Scotch terrier with a letter in his mouth, on page 99. This sketch,

FIG. 95.—HIGH LIFE (1829).

as it is, would form no unworthy companion to one of the most exquisite little etchings ever produced, viz., one of her Majesty's favourite Scotch terrier Islay, begging, executed by Sir Edwin and bit in by his brother, Mr. Thomas Landseer, in the presence of the Queen. This was one of the most rapid pieces of work that ever Sir Edwin accomplished. Instead of being little more than an outline, like Fig. 87, every tuft of its coat is finished to the highest degree, and yet he was but thirty minutes in completing it, and in ten minutes more the plate was ready for printing.

But we have not yet mentioned the aspect most special to the artist in which he regarded dogs, viz., as reflecting human feelings and character. Of the sorrowful reflections we have already said enough in the course of this and other chapters, and it is as a humorist only that we wish to regard Sir Edwin now. Of the many points in which Hogarth and Landseer seem to us to meet there is none more decided (as might be expected) than in humour; but they meet as artists and not as men, as will be seen at once by the portraits of Hogarth with his dog and Sir Edwin with his dogs, each drawn by the artist himself. The trenchant look of Hogarth's unsympathetic face is not more different from the kindly intelligence of Landseer's, than Hogarth's cynical

FIG. 96.—THE RESCUE (1834).

pug from Landseer's good-tempered connoisseurs. The one was a satirist in grain, the other a humorist only. The one was always deeply, almost savagely, in earnest, cutting down to the bone of society, like a moral surgeon; the other did not even try to cut, he did not even treat diseases; he was only a spectator of human life, and only cared to draw such follies as were amusing, and to draw them in such a way that the satirised could join in the laugh. In the picture of "Alexander and Diogenes" the group of canine flatterers comes nearest to the visitors at the levee scene in the "Marriage à la Mode" of any picture with which we are acquainted, both in the variety of social folly expressed, and the perfectness of the expression; but the spirits of the two works are as wide asunder as the poles. In this picture Landseer has shown with

A DANDIE DINMONT (1842).

EOS AND CAIRNACH (1844).

PLATE XXXV.

his greatest power the likeness that exists between human and canine character. Except in the two scandal-mongers, who are evidently indulging in remarks which no dog could even *seem* to make, there is no figure in the picture which might not be a photograph from real life. Dogs look quite as bullying and supercilious as the Alexander, quite as wise as the Diogenes, quite as cringing as the spaniels, quite as solemn and inane as the bloodhounds. Landseer has only put them together. There is undoubtedly satire in showing that our fine airs and pride and wisdom can be so well imitated by dogs; but it is a satire at which we can all afford to laugh, because the wisdom is ridiculed as much as the folly, and the whole thing is evidently

FIG. 97.—ON THE BEACH (1840).

a little play for our amusement. In the "Jack in Office" the satire is a little deeper in the "Jack," whose "insolence of office" is, in its vulgarity and conceit and selfishness, a lesson which we might well take to heart, if it were not for the fact that he is quite right in keeping watch on his master's property, and that the curs that surround his barrow are cowardly thieves. This spoils the lesson of the picture as a whole, and leaves it what it was intended to be—a thing of mirth.

To be considered a satirist in a true sense we think Landseer has no claim; but in drawing mirth from the analogies between human and canine life and human and canine expression, there was no limit to his talent. What can be more humorous,

F F

in a quiet way, than his "Highland Breakfast"—where the common needs of man and brute are shown in the mother suckling her little one, and the puppy, whose mother is drinking with other dogs out of a large pan of milk, is getting its natural breakfast at the same time. In "Highland Music" we have a contrast or strife of sound between dogs and man—the former with their natural voices, the latter with his bagpipes, trying which can make the most noise. Like Hogarth's "Distressed Musician," it almost makes one deaf to look at it. What man of us, or indeed woman, has not sympathized with the scapegrace terrier in "Be it ever so humble there's no place like home," who has been "out on the loose," and come back to his kennel to find his supper stolen? He seems to feel the weight of his iniquity and the comfort of a tub where he can lay down his tired head in peace. Though the home is humble

FIG. 98.—THE FISHERMAN'S DOG: HASTINGS (1840).

it is safe, and, if he had only stayed there, he would have had some supper, however poor. How much to be envied is the snail, who never knows the temptation of "straying," but carries her kennel on the top of her back! In "Dignity and Impudence" the smile is equally ready at a contrast of character so truly human; and in "Laying down the Law" the natural solemnity of the poodle and the accidental resemblance of his ears to a wig, heightened by the close-shaving of the rest of his body except the tufts by his forefeet, which look like ruffled shirt-cuffs, only need the book and spectacles to produce a parody of "the Bench," not so realistic and savage as Hogarth's, but sufficiently striking to amuse us. We might multiply the instances, if it were necessary; but the power of Landseer as a kindly humorist (what we might call a "good-humorist") and as a painter of dogs in all aspects is so well and widely known that further remark would be superfluous. Landseer has been called the "Shakespeare" of dogs, and it is seldom that so bold a comparison is so well justified ; and, considering how often of late we have seen comparisons made between the great poet and modern writers, we may add, that it is seldom the name of Shakespeare is so little taken in vain.

FIG. 99.—EOS,' CAIRNACH, AND A DANDIE DINMONT (1841).

FIG. 100.—NEAR THE FINISH (1820).

CHAPTER VII.

DEER.

I F the dog had the greater share of Landseer's affection, to the deer it remained to affect most deeply his imagination. With the dog were associated all that is most pleasant, most sociable, most affecting to the individual. In his business or his leisure, his moods of mirth and sadness, from his boyhood to his end, the dog was his friend, his companion, his helper, his critic, his jester, his sympathizer, and his mourner. In the field, in the glen, on the mountain or the moor, at the seaside, on his travels, by his bedside, in his dreams of the olden time, wherever or at whatever time men lived and loved and died, the dog had his place as a necessary complement to humanity. But in his thoughts of time and eternity, in the metaphysical puzzles of this world, in the philosophical view of the conditions of this life, the struggle for existence, the meting of pain and pleasure, the inscrutable decrees of Providence, the hopes and fears and theories of existence, the dog gave place to the deer and the eagle, and the wild scenery of their home.

We are compelled to add the scenery, because the deer by itself, in a menagerie or a park, would have had no spiritual influence on Landseer's mind. It was the mystery

AT REST (1826—7).

A DEAD HIND (1827).

PLATE XXXVI.

of the mountains and the clouds and mists of Scotland, the awfulness of their solitude, the terror of their sudden and magnificent displays of Nature's power, their incomprehensibility, their defiance of the power of man, their sacred splendour of light and shade and colour, that made the deer and the eagle, to whom this almost supernatural world was a home and a condition of existence, the animals which of all others were the most suggestive of thought as to the relations between the Maker and the made, and that boundless history of man, in which the history of the individual is but an atom.

But this was not always so. These far-reaching thoughts were the result of the

FIG. 101.—MOUNTING GUARD (1828).*

broodings of years, in which he paid his visits to Scotland as a sportsman and an artist. Of all sports, deerstalking was that of which he was most fond. It was a battle, he used to say, between the intelligence of man and brute. How much he loved it, both as an artist and sportsman, is shown by his almost innumerable sketches of some

---

* A lithograph of this was published in "Harding's Use of the Black Lead Pencil." The drawing is in pen and ink.

scene or other connected with it, to say nothing of the magnificent series of pictures
which, year after year, sometimes by twos and threes, used to gladden the eyes of the
visitors to the Royal Academy. Of his two series of drawings mainly relating to the
stag ("The Forest" and "Deerstalking"), one was entirely devoted to different scenes
connected with the sport: "Watching the Body," "How to get the Deer Home,"
"The Poacher's Bothy," "The Last Scene," "The Combat," and "Waiting for the
Deer." But his delight was greater as an artist than as a sportsman. Mr. Stephens

FIG. 102.—FALLOW DEER (1838).

says, "People naturally fancied Sir Edwin was a keen sportsman. Nevertheless, such
was by no means the case. In truth, he often carried the gun as an introduction to the
sketch-book." And he tells two stories in corroboration of his opinion, one of which
shows only that Sir Edwin was not considered a good shot, but the other is to the
point. "On another occasion the gillies were astonished, just as a magnificent shot
came in the way, to have Sir Edwin's gun thrust into their hands, with ' Here, take
—take this!' hastily ejaculated, while the sketch-book was pulled out for shot of a

Deer (1830)

Stag and Hind (1850).

Plate XXXVII.

different fashion." "The gillies," adds Mr. Stephens, "were often much disgusted by being led about the moors, walking, with more sketching than shooting."

He was, therefore, interested in deer both as an artist and a sportsman, but rather as an artist; and to these points of view must be added another, we think, as constant as either of the others—viz., as a man. He always loved the dog, and he always pitied the deer. It was, as we have formerly observed, the only animal, the object of sport, in whose fate he sympathized. Rats might be killed, and a good riddance to them; partridges and pheasants were shot, and there was an end to them; cats and rabbits and hares might suggest an exclamation of patronising sympathy; but there was no righteous delight about the fall of a deer, no patronage in the pity which it caused. As a sportsman it was the result of a match worthy of both, as an artist it

FIG. 103.—AT PLAY (1838).

was an incident of grandeur as well as beauty, as a man it was a sight of almost pure pain at the sad havoc of a noble creature—little less than a catastrophe.

Nevertheless, the artist was king of all, and compelled him to draw the match, the incident, and the catastrophe, with the same faultless truth. Of the catastrophe, there is scarcely any drawing of Landseer's of a dead deer in which the sentiment is not suggested, and we have called attention to this in our comments on what must have been almost his first drawings of the dead animal (Figs. 35 and 36). The artist also compelled him to draw things almost repugnant to the man, such as the "Grealoch," or the habit dogs have of licking the deer's wounds. We have also noticed the fact that he began to make studies of the deer before he visited their natural home, or engaged in the sports of stalking or driving, viz., in 1820, when he drew the originals of Figs. 21 and 32. One other study of this year we give as the headpiece to this chapter. ("Near the Finish," Fig. 100), in which the dogs are more like deerhounds than in Fig. 32; but which shows, as do both the former drawings, that the deer had already excited his imagination, and that he already sympathized rather with the pursued than the pursuer. There is a helpless limp about the hindquarters in all three drawings which is pathetic. The dying stag and the dead hind in PLATE XXXVI. both convey similar sentiments, one of sorrow for the pain of the noble and innocent, and the other of pity for the beautiful dead. Both these and "Mounting Guard" (Fig. 101) are comparatively early drawings.

How far less interest the tame deer in a park had for Landseer than the wild animal of the forest, is plainly shown in "Fallow Deer" (Fig. 102), and the two slight

FIG. 104.—IN THE PARK (1842).

sketches "At Play" and "In the Park" (Figs. 103 and 104), in which the artist seems to have been as much "at play" as the deer, and to have tried to make his work as uninteresting to us as it was to him. There is not even the beauty of grouping so observable in his most ordinary sketches; and we may as well here dismiss with a word the unfinished drawing of a "Stag's Head" (Fig. 105) and the "Hinds' Heads" (Fig. 109), the latter of which, however, deserves to be placed in the same rank as the rams' heads and bison in PLATES XXVII. and XXVIII., for beauty and power of execution.

The deer was the only animal of which Landseer may be said to have made a special study in its wild state, and whose natural life he may be said to have watched

THE ALARM.

A DRIVE OF DEER : GLEN ORCHAY.

PLATE XXXVIII.

with never-wearying care and pleasure. The beauty of its form, the nobility and grace of its bearing, the cleverness of its instincts, and its courage in extremity, together with the sublimity of its home, gave it a fascination from which Landseer never escaped. The grand isolated being, with so much for man to love and admire, and yet so totally beyond the range of his influence, so gentle and so wild, and within the circle of whose existence man never comes but to destroy, has quite enough in itself to attract the artist or poet without any effort of the imagination or excitement of sport. Landseer may be said to have mastered other animals, but the deer mastered him. He raised dogs almost to the scale of humanity, but deer raised him to a level of higher being. His love for the deer may not have been so deep, but

FIG. 105.—STAG'S HEAD (1842).

it was more elevating, less self-regarding, and it ended at last in stimulating his imagination to produce pictures deeper in thought and more awful in sentiment than any attempted by an animal painter before.

But this was the result of a long study of the deer and of nature for their own sake—the true motive of the artist, and far higher than his pictures of deerstalking, although this sport gave rise to such beautiful works as "Crossing the Bridge" and "A Drive of Deer" (of the latter of which we give a woodcut on PLATE XXXVIII.) we rank those of which the motive is rather the natural habits and character of the deer than the "pleasures of the chase." Of this class of study we give so many examples in this chapter as will make reference needless to those larger works which are so well known by engravings, such as "None but the Brave deserve the Fair,"

and "The Challenge," and "The Monarch of the Glen." The first of these is
"Suspicion" (Fig. 106), in which a herd of deer are startled by some taint in the air
or noise on the wind. This, with the two following figures (107 and 108)—"Missed"
and "Doomed"—are taken from the artist's drawings from his own work of "The
Forest"—a series of twenty drawings, for which it was originally intended that Lord
Alexander Russell should write the letterpress.* On PLATE XXXVII. will be found
two finished studies—the one of roe, and the other of red deer—specially interesting
both for their beauty and finish, and also because they were executed by Sir Edwin
and etched by Mr. Thomas Landseer for the Queen's letter and note-paper. On

FIG. 106.—SUSPICION (1852).

the next plate (XXXVIII.) is a woodcut from an oil-picture ("The Alarm"), also of
great beauty; on the next (XXXIX.), a study of the heads of two stags fighting
("The Combat"), and another called "The Challenge"—the former of which was
probably sketched for the author's series of "Deerstalking," and the latter as a study
for the well-known picture of the same name, or for the "Stag bellowing"—a picture
of 1845 not engraved.

The engravings to this chapter will do much towards showing the power of the
artist as a draughtsman of deer. They show the wonderful force and beauty with

_____

* Graves, p. 31.

which he drew the form; one feels impressed with it as with an actual presence, so consummately felt is each figure in all its qualities, whether of fullness of life, or strength of limb, or bulk or weight of body, or harmony of organization. Each figure needs little to make it a splendid study for the sculptor, like his own magnificent model of a "Stag at Bay," exhibited at the Royal Academy in 1866. They also show the accuracy and care with which he studied their various attitudes and habits. They reflect their sensitiveness and their grace, their timidity towards man, and their courage between themselves. They also show something of the loneliness

FIG. 107.—MISSED.

of their haunts, their care of their young, and even—in Fig. 109—the texture of their hair and the consistency of their noses and ears; but they give but a faint notion of the beauty and impressiveness of the landscapes with which they were surrounded in his pictures, or of the lofty sentiment with which the grandest of these were inspired. To do this we need the pictures themselves, or such true interpretation of them as the best engravings can give, which yet lose much from want of colour and from imperfect translation of his chiaroscuro. Landseer has, however, been singularly fortunate in his engravers, among whom we may specially mention Mr. Outrim, Mr. C. G. Lewis, and Mr. Samuel Cousins, R.A., whose plate of "The

Midsummer Night's Dream," with its wonderful white rabbit, is so well known.
Chief, however, among his engravers must ever stand his brother, Thomas Landseer,
not only on account of the quantity but the quality of his engraving. And of all
his plates most wonderful to us seem those of "Night" and "Morning," for the
perfect rendering not only of form but of sentiment. They are more like the best
etchings than engravings, so sympathetically does his touch alter to express every
difference of texture, even to the imitation of the artist's handling of the fur of the
fox or the coats of the deer; but more marvellous still is the perfectness with which

Fig. 108.—Doomed.

aërial effects are produced—the transparency of the clouds, the mystery of the mists.
The tonality is so perfect that one scarcely misses the colour, which indeed may almost
be said to be given.

Who amongst us has not felt the poetical magic of these later pictures of deer,
in which the artist seems to contemplate their life with a sadness like that of Jacques,
but without its humour? There was never any suggestion of mirth to Landseer in
relation to the deer. In these pictures he seems to look upon them from the sad hill
of philosophy, whence he sees their history and sufferings as a sorrowful example of
the strange inconsistencies of the lot of all created beings. In the "Challenge,"

THE COMBAT (1844).

A CHALLENGE (1845).

PLATE XXXIX.

and "Night" and "Morning," we have the three scenes of the tragedy of life: first, the desire of supremacy and possession that will brook no rival, the lustiness of strength, the fatal attraction of beauty; in the second, the terrible struggle for life; the strange ordinance that requires that the happiness of one cannot be consummated without the destruction of another; that two noble beings must set their hearts upon the same object, and that one must die that the other may be content; and thirdly, the end of all earthly hopes—the final tragedy in the death, not of one, but of both, and the unpitying regard of nature for the noblest of her handiwork, who leaves the lifeless forms to moulder on the moor and to be the portion of foxes.

FIG. 109.—HINDS' HEADS.

I 1

FIG. 110.—HIGHLANDER AND PONIES (1827).

CHAPTER VIII.

HORSES.

ROM the early sketches by Landseer in the fields near Hampstead of the various animals which he found pasturing there—the cows, the sheep, and the horses—one would have expected to find them playing more prominent parts in his compositions; but we find in after years the interest of man and dogs and deer swept them, not exactly off the stage, but into the obscurity of supernumeraries. That this should have been the case with other cattle we could more easily have understood; for, though they are of great value with regard to form and colour in a composition, their characters are so limited and their gift of expression so little in comparison with the dogs and the deer, that they could not but suffer in competition. It is, however, very different with the horse, whose beauty yields to that of no other animal, whose devotion to man is almost as great as the dog's, and whose variety of disposition and utility is as remarkable as the variations of its form; and yet, instead of finding it in a superior place in Landseer's art, we find it neglected more than any other animal. By neglect we do not mean that he ever ceased to draw it, or to draw it well; but that it more rarely formed a centre of interest in his compositions, and that those compositions in which it formed the centre of interest were little more than portrait groups.

And yet what patience he took to master its form and habits is fully exemplified in the woodcuts in this volume. In the " Head of a Cart Horse" (Fig. 111) we have a most careful study of the way in which a horse approaches his food with his lips and nose, and in Fig. 112 we have a study of the whole animal, showing accurate observation of the way in which a horse stands with his head weighed down by a heavy nosebag, and with the sleepy look of contentment which characterizes it when engaged in chumping grain. In PLATE VI. ("On the Common") we find that in the

FIG. 111.—HEAD OF A CART HORSE (1815).

three years which have elapsed since Fig. 112, he has learnt to draw and fore-shorten the animal with perfect skill. From that time forward he scarcely makes any further progress, or represents the animal in any other light than a simple figure remarkable for its beauty or its usefulness, but without any special character of its own that engages our attention strongly. It may surprise and delight us with the fullness of its beauty, the gloss of its coat, and its evident gentleness of disposition, as in the picture of "Shoeing the Bay Mare;" we may admire its exquisite grace of curve in the "Indian Tent, Mare and Foal;" but we feel that in both these cases the artist has been but feebly interested in the character of the animal, and cares far more about the beauty of its skin and its effect in the composition than its life and essential qualities as a horse. He painted "Taming the Shrew," or, rather, he called a picture by this name; but the animal was tamed and the shrew extinguished before he painted her, and she was as tame as the rest of his horses.

In all his works Landseer preferred rest to action. Even his dogs—the most lively of his animals—he usually represented in repose, either standing, sitting, sleeping, or in attitudes of suspense. His deer were sometimes trotting—and how finely he could make them trot when he liked we may see in Fig. 107; they were galloping sometimes, as in the "Drive of Deer" (PLATE XXXVIII.); but in the majority of his

FIG. 112.—A CART HORSE (1815).

pictures they were motionless. Even in his pictures of fighting deer—as in the frightful struggle in "Night"—opposing forces have produced rest. But the most motionless of all his animals are his horses. They seldom even move their tails, and if they lift a hoof from the ground it is only to be "shoed." The only cases in which he has painted horses or ponies moving at more than a snail's pace are in his portrait of Lord Cosmo Russell and another of Lord Alexander (PLATE XL.), each on his pony, again in his picture of "Chevy Chase," where there is a real attempt at horselike spirit, and in one hunting sketch.

IN THE STABLE.

LORD ALEXANDER RUSSELL ON EMERALD (1829).

PLATE XL.

Yet his drawings of the horse are admirable, as far as they go. As a picture of beauty of horse-form we know nothing to equal his "bay mare." It is easy to criticize its shortcomings by enumerating qualities which it was never intended to possess; but at the end of all it remains impressed on the retina of the mind as a beautiful thing, which once seen can never be altogether lost from the memory. It is not only the glossiness of her coat or the exquisite beauty of her shape, but she has a nobility of bearing which raises her to the equine aristocracy, and makes us easily believe that to be tied up while she was being shoed, like an ordinary, underbred, uncultivated

FIG. 113.—A FARM TEAM (1818).

mare, was an insult not to be borne.* His Highland ponies, as in Fig. 36, Fig. 43, and PLATE XXIX., are knowing and shrewd, and as well understood in form as

---

* Mr. Bell (to whom the bay mare, Betty, belonged) gives the following account of the picture in his Catalogue. "It has been reported that the mare would not stand to be shod unless in company with a donkey. The truth is, that the intimacy of the mare and the donkey commenced in the studio, and was cemented on the canvas. Another rumour states that the scene, as painted, occurred in the forge of a country blacksmith, where the mare was having a shoe fastened, and that the painter was so pleased with the composition that he made an elaborate sketch for the picture on the spot. Some critics have noticed the 'oversight' of the mare having no bridle or halter. This was not an oversight, as she would stand to be shod or cleaned without being fastened, but had a great objection to be tied up in a forge or against a post or door. When this has been attempted she often started back with a sudden jerk and broke the bridle. Other critics have remarked that from the mode of painting the toe of the off fore-foot, the mare appears as if her weight rested only on two legs. This was noticed before the picture was finished, and she was placed in position several times for the purpose of ensuring accuracy. In every instance she placed the foot exactly in the position represented."—Graves, p. 26.

K K

any of his animals, while in his studies during his tour abroad in 1840 he wrought
the foreign animals with marvellous readiness and character.   Indeed, we have
never seen a drawing of a horse by Landseer without wishing to see another,
or wondering why he allowed all the animation and action of the animal always to
remain, as it were, in solution.   The wonder and the regret increase when we turn to
such a picture as "The Horse Fair," and see how grand a sight can be made of the
ordinary but continual strife for mastery that is going on between the human and
equine wills.   Nor do they lessen when we see a picture so full of the force of animal
life as "The Council of Horses," by James Ward, R.A., an artist who still stands

FIG. 114.—WAITING ON THE ROAD (1824).

unrivalled amongst British artists in the vigour and truth with which he represented
the native spirit of the brute.   Landseer's horses have no wills of their own : they are
all well broken and subdued to the service of their masters.   His feeling towards the
horse seems to have been simply a delight in its beauty, and a pleasure in seeing it
happily, if somewhat stupidly, at rest.   Nearly all our figures of his horses are in the
same position—standing at ease, with their bodies well thrown forward to take the
weight off the hind legs, as is the manner of horses.   We see this in the "Highlander
and Ponies" (Fig. 110), "A Cart Horse" (Fig. 112), "Highlander and Horses"
(Figs. 115 and 116), and "In the Stable" (PLATE XL.).   We do not see it in Fig. 113,

because the horses are ill drawn (we fancy that the date ascribed to this sketch must be erroneous, as it is far behind other sketches of the same and earlier dates in knowledge and execution, if we judge by our woodcuts), and we do not see it in Fig. 114, because the man hides the shoulders. All the late sketches are remarkable for their ease and mastery, and Fig. 116 shows great feeling of the beauty of the heads and necks; but, as a whole, they are less interesting than any others of his sketches —more wanting in vigour and variety. There is a sense of sameness quite foreign to his other work, although the groups are very varied in composition.

One reason for this comparative neglect of one of the noblest and most beautiful of animals may be found in the preference shown by Landseer for the sports of Scotland to those of England. He did not hunt, and he did not race, and though he

FIG. 115.—HIGHLANDER AND HORSES (1827).

could ride he preferred to walk, as was natural to an artist; and another reason is that he could not do everything; and seeing how richly we have profited by his devotion to the dog and the deer we may well be thankful for what we have got, without complaining that he did not put forth his full strength in his pictures of horses. But we wish he had painted Rosinante.

But it was not the horse alone that was neglected. The pig—one of his earliest favourites—was condemned to complete oblivion, and his bulls, which he drew in his boyhood with such vigour, were relegated with cows to the minor rôles—mere pieces of utility, to be introduced now and again for effect of form or colour, but never with any proper recognition of their special qualities or brute feelings. While we, with regard to them, would use the same argument as with regard to horses, viz., that Landseer could not do everything, we yet may be allowed to regret that he painted no picture which of its kind can compare with the ".Fighting Bulls" of James Ward, or even the splendid group of bull, cow, and calf by the same artist in the National Gallery, and the more so as he showed in his youth the power to add this laurel to his fame, if he had so minded.

His laurels, however, are thick enough without this : he painted dogs and deer as no man ever painted them before ; he inspired one with a humour and both with a poetry beyond all parallel in art ; he added to this a feeling for the grandeur and

FIG. 116.—HIGHLANDER AND HORSES (1827).

sublimity of nature which gave to his pictures a charm and a sentiment which all can feel ; he never painted anything false or ignoble, vulgar or unmanly ; he won, as an artist purely, the affection and admiration of a whole people as scarcely any man, not a poet, or a soldier, or a statesman, or a philosopher, has ever won them before ; and if against these achievements, to which many more may be added, we say that there were some animals which he chiefly regarded in their picturesque aspects, it is not much.

THE END.

LONDON : PRINTED BY VIRTUE AND CO., LIMITED, CITY ROAD.

www.ingramcontent.com/pod-product-compliance
Lightning Source LLC
Chambersburg PA
CBHW030324270326
41926CB00010B/1498